ON POETRY AND STYLE

The Library of Liberal Arts

OSKAR PIEST, FOUNDER

. . . .

ON POETRY
AND STYLE

ARISTOTLE

Translated, with an introduction, by
G. M. A. GRUBE
Professor of Classics, Trinity College
University of Toronto

The Library of Liberal Arts
published by

Macmillan Publishing Company
New York
Collier Macmillan Publishers
London

Macmillan Publishing Company
866 Third Avenue
New York, New York 10022

First Edition
Twenty-second Printing — 1986

Library of Congress Catalog Card Number: 58-13827
ISBN 0-02-348500-0

CONTENTS

EDITOR'S INTRODUCTION ix

SELECTED BIBLIOGRAPHY xxxi

NOTE ON THE TEXT xxxii

ARISTOTLE ON POETRY AND STYLE

THE POETICS

CHAPTER I 3

Poetry as Imitation (3), Differences in Means of Imitation (3), No Greek Word for Literature (4)

CHAPTER II 5

Differences in Models of Imitation (5)

CHAPTER III 6

Differences in Manner of Imitation (6), Dorian Claims (6)

CHAPTER IV 7

The Origins of Poetry (7), The History of Tragedy (8)

CHAPTER V 10

The History of Comedy (10), Epic and Tragedy: Unity of Time (11)

CHAPTER VI 11

The Definition of Tragedy (11), The Six Elements or Aspects of Tragedy (12), Plot and Character (13), Thought and Character (14), Diction, Music, Spectacle (15)

CHAPTER VII 15

Plot: Beginning, Middle, and End (15), Size or Length (16)

CHAPTER VIII 17
Unity of Plot (17)

CHAPTER IX 18
Tragedy and History (18), Names of Characters:
Traditional Legends (18), Types of Plots (20)

CHAPTER X 20
Simple and Complex Plots (20)

CHAPTER XI 21
Reversals and Recognitions (21)

CHAPTER XII 23
The Sections of a Tragedy (23)

CHAPTER XIII 23
Possible Changes of Fortune (23), The Tragic
Character (24), The Best Plots (24), The Double
Plot of Comedy (25)

CHAPTER XIV 26
Pity and Fear should be due to Plot, not to
Spectacle (26), The Tragic Situation (27), Acting
in Ignorance (27)

CHAPTER XV 29
Four Aims in Characterization (29), The Supernatural (31), Characterization (31), Care for Details
of Presentation (32)

CHAPTER XVI 32
Kinds of Recognition (32)

CHAPTER XVII 34
Need to Visualize the Play (34), Emotions of the
Dramatist (34), The Outline (35)

CHAPTER XVIII 36
Involvement and Unraveling (36), Four Types of
Tragedy (36), Epic and Tragic Plots (38), Defective
Plots (38), The Chorus (39)

CHAPTER XIX 40
Thought (40), Diction: Modes of Expression (40)

CHAPTER XX 41
The Parts of Speech (41)

CHAPTER XXI 44
Compound Words and Metaphors (44)

CHAPTER XXII 46
Excellence of Diction (46)

CHAPTER XXIII 49
The Epic (49)

CHAPTER XXIV 50
The Epic—continued (50), The Marvelous and the Inexplicable (53)

CHAPTER XXV 54
Problems of Criticism (54), Intrinsic and Incidental Flaws (55), Poetry and Truth (56), The Representation of Evil (56), Criticisms of Diction (56), The Right Critical Attitude (59)

CHAPTER XXVI 61
Tragedy and Epic (61)

RHETORIC [BOOK THREE, *Chapters I-XII*]

CHAPTER I 65
History of Style and Delivery (66)

CHAPTER II 68
The Right Diction (68), The Metaphor (70), Importance of Words (72)

CHAPTER III 73
Causes of Frigidity (73)

CHAPTER IV 75
Similes (75)

CHAPTER V 76
Five Requirements of Style (76)

CHAPTER VI 79
A Weighty Style (79)

CHAPTER VII 80
Appropriateness (80)

CHAPTER VIII 82
Prose Rhythm (82)

CHAPTER IX 84
Sentence Structure: the Period (84), Antithesis (86),
Parisosis and Paromoiosis (87)

CHAPTER X 88
Happy Phrases (88), Examples of Metaphors (90)

CHAPTER XI 92
The Active Metaphor (92), Examples of Wit (94),
Proverbs (96), Hyperboles (96)

CHAPTER XII 97
Variations in Style (97), Asyndeton (98), Three
Kinds of Rhetoric (99)

BRIEF SUMMARY OF CHAPTERS XIII-XIX 100

BIOGRAPHICAL INDEX 101

ARISTOTLE AS A LITERARY CRITIC

I

Greek criticism of literature begins for us when Xenophanes and Heraclitus, around 500 B.C., violently attacked Homer for telling immoral and untrue stories about the gods. This was the beginning of what Plato called "the ancient quarrel between poetry and philosophy." [1] He was, of course, himself writing in that tradition when he banished the poets, or at least most of them, from his ideal state. This concern with the moral and social effects and social values of literature is quite legitimate; in a society like ancient Athens where poetry was itself a potent social force, it was inevitable; it becomes a "moral fallacy" in criticism only when social and artistic criteria are confused.

Greek criticism often did confuse them. When Aristophanes in his *Frogs* (405 B.C.) staged a contest between Aeschylus and Euripides for the Chair of Tragedy in Hades, moral and artistic criticisms were inextricably mingled, yet many of his objections to Euripidean tragedy were purely artistic in nature. Plato, however, saw the distinction between criticism of content and of form quite clearly,[2] and he was the first to formulate a number of basic principles of literary criticism—as for example, that every literary work, whether in prose or verse, must have an organic structure, with a place for each of its parts, every part in its place and in its proper relation to every other part and to the whole. He insisted on the difference be-

[1] *Republic* 607b. Xenophanes, fragm. 11: "Homer and Hesiod attributed to the gods all the things which, among mortals, bring blame and shame: theft, adultery, and deception." Heraclitus, in fragm. 42, says that Homer should for this reason be excluded from competitions and thrashed.

[2] *Phaedrus* 236a; also 264b-d for the insistence on organic unity; and 268a-269d for the difference between art and technique.

tween art and technique. In the *Laws* he sought the origin of *mousikē* (poetry and music) in a gift of the gods to man: the sense of rhythm and harmony. He established three criteria of good art: its moral effect, the pleasure it gives, and "the correctness of its imitation." This last is somewhat crudely formulated, but it is at least an artistic criterion.[3]

However angry critics and poets have been with Plato for his attacks on poetry, no sensible critic has ever denied that he was himself a very great literary artist and a poet. No one, on the other hand, would make any such claim for Aristotle on the basis of his extant works.[4] Indeed, it is a curious paradox of literary history that the author of probably the most famous, and certainly the most influential, critical work on poetry had, quite obviously, very little feeling for poetry, and a much more restricted view of its importance than his predecessor. This does not detract from Aristotle's contribution to criticism, but it does mean that, in order to understand that contribution, we must not ignore the philosopher's somewhat curious attitude.

Poetry was, to Aristotle, "more philosophic" than history, but it always remained much inferior to philosophy itself.[5] There is more than a touch of superciliousness in his treatment of poetry, of style, of literature in general. The effect of this attitude is at times startling, as when we find the author of the *Poetics* writing in his *Politics* (5. 8. 20) that the rich

3 *Laws* 2. 653c-654a, and my *Plato's Thought* (London, 1935, repr. Beacon Press, Boston, 1958), pp. 179-215, for a full discussion of Plato's theories of art. For the three criteria, *Laws* 667b-669b.

4 To the surprise of all modern readers, Cicero (*Acad.* 2. 38) speaks of the golden flow of Aristotle's eloquence, but it is a passage which seems to have in mind content as much as style. Quintilian speaks of his "agreeable" style, *suavitas eloquendi*, but it is a bare reference in a list of his accomplishments, in strong contrast to the almost lyric praise of Plato's "divine and Homeric" artistry (10. 1. 81-83). *Suavitas* is a quality of the middle style, neither deliberately simple nor ornate, which suits some of the works we have, though both Cicero and Quintilian are probably thinking mainly of his lost, more popular, dialogues. The contrast with Plato, even so, is supported by Quintilian.

5 *Poetics* 9 (init.).

should be protected in a democracy and discouraged from wasting their substance on expensive and useless public services "such as dramatic performances, torch races and the like." In the *Rhetoric* (2. 9. 11), speaking of inferior men contending with their betters, he adds: "as, for instance, if a poet or musician (*mousikos*) should contend with a just man, for justice is better than *mousikē*." Remembering such passages, we shall be less surprised to find him saying that style and delivery are really superfluous but must be employed "because of the depravity of the audiences"; or that prose writers at first adopted poetic diction "because the poets, though they said silly things, were thought to have acquired their reputation because of their language"; and he adds that the poets themselves have now come to use simpler language, a process he clearly approves. One also thinks of his advice to avoid ambiguity unless one deliberately seeks it, "which is what people do who have nothing to say but pretend that they have. Such people usually write poetry, as Empedocles did." There is surely an undertone of irony where he says that unnecessary epithets—e.g., "white milk"—are appropriate in poetry but should be avoided in prose, and also in his advice that, to achieve a weighty style, one should not say "circle," but speak, instead, of "a two-dimensional figure equidistant from the center." [6]

Such passages with their dry humor should remind us that Aristotle does not get excited about poetry, not even about tragedy, whereas Plato could not mention poetry without emotion because of the perpetual conflict within himself between the poet and the philosopher. In Aristotle there is no conflict; the philosopher is always firmly in command and the poet is nonexistent. Aristotle brings to bear upon poetry and style his tremendously powerful analytic mind, as he brought it to bear upon almost every department of human activity and human life. The result is the *Poetics,* a work which contains the first formulation of some extraordinarily seminal

[6] For these quotations from the *Rhetoric* 3. 1, 5 and 6, see pp. 66-68 and 79 below.

ideas which are at the very root of our appreciation of poetry, and of tragedy in particular—ideas which have continued to grow and to develop. It is a sufficient proof of his greatness that he was the first to grasp such ideas, even though, being the first, he could neither see their implications fully nor perfectly express them. These ideas have been pondered and refined for centuries; it does not help our understanding either of poetry or of the history of literary appreciation to try to read these modern refinements into Aristotle's words. Moreover, because Aristotle was handicapped by lack of poetic feeling, he seems to miss, at times, what to us appears of the very essence of poetry. In his analysis of prose style, where feeling is less important, we feel less frustrated. There he has put down some basic principles which are as valid today as they were in the fourth century B.C.—but of course he had his prejudices: "No one teaches geometry that way"! [7]

Aristotle is never at his best when he is arguing, and especially when he is arguing against Plato. Now Plato had maintained that the epic was superior to tragedy.[8] Aristotle holds the contrary opinion (in either case the comparison is rather futile), and unfortunately it affects his whole treatment of the epic in the *Poetics*. This culminates in chapter 26 where he finally proves to his own satisfaction the superiority of tragedy. It is usually said that the *Poetics* deals with poetry, with tragedy in particular, and with the epic to a lesser extent. It would be a truer description to say that the *Poetics* (as we have it) treats of tragedy, with incidental remarks on poetry in general, and on some other poetic genres, particularly the epic, as compared with tragedy. Aristotle has told us himself that every poetic genre has its own *dynamis,* its own force and function.[9] But he reduces the epic to an inferior kind of tragedy which serious-minded men abandoned in its favor once tragedy had been developed. It has only four elements

[7] *Rhetoric* 3. 1, p. 67 below.

[8] *Laws* 2. 658d.

[9] In the first sentence of the *Poetics;* for tragedy as the later form than epic see ch. 4.

instead of six, but it can be classified roughly into the same types; it is less compact and economic; the unity of its plots is looser. He even hints that the Homeric epic was too long and suggests as a standard length that of three, or possibly four, tragedies (a whole epic could then also be recited in a day). He makes no attempt to analyze the epic in itself, he does not define it or the special pleasure it gives, nor does he try to discover its special beauties and special appeal. Here and there he does make some interesting remarks on the epic—its capacity to use the supernatural, for example. That Aristotle will always do on any subject; he also has Homer very much in mind, and frequently illustrates his thoughts *on tragedy* from Homer. It is important to grasp the context of such remarks on the epic as we find in the *Poetics,* if only to understand why they seem so very unsatisfying. The comparison of tragedy with history is another example of the same tendency. There, too, Aristotle is looking at tragedy and he does not bother to look squarely at history at all.

Aristotle's method is analytic: he always gazes intently at the object of his particular inquiry. Plato's method is synoptic: he cannot discuss poetry, or prose literature for that matter, without forever thinking of their purpose and function in society, so that social values always obtrude. Aristotle keeps within the limits he has set himself in any particular treatise; the social value of poetry—the moral outlook—therefore remains in the background unless it is being specifically discussed. It is so treated once, at the end of the *Politics,* where *mousikē* (music *and* poetry) is discussed with its uses and functions in society in view, and there the point of view is thoroughly Platonic.[10]

10 *Politics* 8. 5-7. The standard translations of Benjamin Jowett (Oxford, 1916) and Ernest Barker (Oxford, 1946) render *mousikē* throughout the discussion of education by "music," whereas it refers to music *and poetry*, as is natural in such a context. In certain sections, and particularly in ch. 6, where he discusses which musical modes are to be used in education, Aristotle has music *mainly* in mind, but not exclusively. That *mousikē* has the general meaning should be clear from several passages. At 1337b 24-5 education is said to consist of letters (i.e., reading and

He there approaches the subject in the same way that Plato did in the *Republic*.[11] His rulers must see to it that only stories with a good moral are told to children; they must not tolerate bad language; strict censorship is to be exercised over painting, poetry, and sculpture. Comedy, because it is sanctioned by custom, will be tolerated but witnessed only by adult males.

The last three chapters of the *Politics* discuss the educational value of *mousikê*.[12] It has three functions: (1) it contributes to the recreation of adults, (2) it trains character, (3) it contributes to the life of leisure—a life reached by only a few men for brief periods of time. We might call these the recreational, the educational, and the cultural functions of poetry and music. Unfortunately, Aristotle says no more about the last. He had made an important distinction between

---

writing), physical training, and *mousikê*, to which some add drawing. That Aristotle should here omit poetry is quite unthinkable; it is obviously included in *mousikê*. He then deals with physical training in ch. 4, and with *mousikê* in 5-7. At 1339b 20 *mousikê* with or without *melôdia* does *not* mean "music, whether instrumental or accompanied by the voice" (Barker) or "music . . . whether with or without song" (Jowett), but "poetry with or without song" (i.e., with or without music). Again, at 1340a 13 we are told that "all men are roused to sympathy when they listen to imitations, even without rhythm or tune." This does not mean "mere imitative sounds" (Barker), whatever they might be; imitation without rhythm or tune is prose (as compared to poetry, it may be said to have no rhythm, i.e., no meter), and Aristotle means that men are affected even by imitative speeches. And when we are told, at 1340a 18, that "rhythm and melody give imitations . . . of anger, gentleness, courage, moderation . . . and other ethical qualities" and that "our soul changes as we listen to them," this obviously includes poetry and drama, and Aristotle still includes them when he says that only through our sense of hearing are we so affected, for he is obviously thinking of words as well as tunes (1340a 20). Nor can "the *mousikê* in the theater" or "the spectator" (1342a 18) exclude drama. As this is the only discussion of *mousikê* in society it is important to realize clearly what Aristotle is discussing.

11 Cp. *Politics* 7. 17. 5-10 (1336a 30-b. 35) with *Republic* 3. 376e-378a. Note that at b16 Aristotle takes the theory of art as imitation for granted.

12 *Politics* 8. 3. 2-6 (1337b 28-1338a 13).

recreation and leisure: play is necessary to refresh and re-create us after work, but leisure is the time which remains after both work and recreation. The proper use of leisure is essential to the happy life, but Aristotle nowhere explains the contribution which *mousikē* can make to it. This is all the more to be regretted because this third function is not found in Plato but is a deliberate addition.

Aristotle then goes on to discuss the emotional effect of *mousikē* upon an audience, and he has two related but differ-ent ideas in mind: *sympatheia* or "feeling with," the emo-tional identification so feared by Plato, and that extreme emotional excitement or ecstasy (*enthousiasmos*) through which *mousikē* may ultimately bring about a catharsis, a purgation of the emotions which restores a more natural and balanced state.[13]

It is in its recreational function that *mousikē* is to have this cathartic effect. Here Aristotle has music mainly in mind (though words may accompany it, as they usually did), and he states that the musical modes to be used for this cathartic purpose are quite different from those that should be used in education. This healing of the emotions (pity, fear, and *enthousiasmos* are specifically mentioned) is directed at those who are emotionally unbalanced. We are then referred to the *Poetics* for a further explanation of catharsis but since if this was ever written it is lost, we should look closely at the key passage of the *Politics*.

> An emotion which strongly affects some souls is present in all to a varying degree, for example pity and fear, and also ecstasy. To this last some people are particularly liable, and we see that under the influence of religious music and songs

[13] *Politics* 8. 7. 3-8 (1341b 33-1342a 29). The beneficial effect of music in "Corybantic healing" is noted also by Plato in the *Laws* (790c 5-791b 2). The disturbances are there said to be a form of fear and are treated homeopathically by working up to a crisis which brings relief. The whole concept of catharsis in Aristotle, its origin in Plato and its relation to Aristotle's psychology and physiology, is fully treated in the extremely enlightening and interesting study by Jeanne Croissant, *Aristote et les Mystères* (Liège, 1932), especially pp. 1-111.

which drive the soul to frenzy, they calm down as if they had been medically treated and purged. People who are given to pity or fear, and emotional people generally, and others to the extent that they have similar emotions, must be affected in the same way; for all of them must experience a kind of purgation and pleasurable relief. In the same way, cathartic (songs and) music give men harmless delight. We must therefore make those who practice *mousikê* in the theater perform these kinds of tunes and songs.

There are two kinds of spectator: the one kind is a free and educated man, the other, the vulgar kind, is made up of mechanics and general laborers and other such people; these too must be provided with contests and spectacles for their recreation. Their souls are perverted from their natural state; so there are perversions of melody and songs that are tense and corrupted. Every man takes pleasure in what is naturally akin to him, and we must therefore allow the performers to use this kind of *mousikê* with this kind of spectator in view.[14]

The meaning of catharsis seems here quite clear. Aristotle is defending some kinds of music and poetry (undoubtedly including tragedy) against Plato, as if he had said to him: "You yourself have said that choral *mousikê*, etc., were granted to men by the gods in order to re-establish their emotional balance which gets disturbed from time to time in adult life.[15] In order to make this possible we must allow emotional, cathartic *mousikê* to be performed, but you, rather illogically if I may say so, banned such *mousikê* from your ideal state." One can imagine him adding: "Of course, this catharsis only

---

14 *Politics* 8. 7. 4 (1342a 5-23).

15 Cf. *Laws* 2. 653a-e. Plato has there defined education as training children to the habit of taking pleasure in the right things which their reason will later approve. He then says: "Now this education which consists in the right feelings of pleasure and pain is frequently slackened and corrupted in the course of human life. The gods felt pity for the human race which is naturally inclined to misery; they established for man the feasts of the gods as periods of rest from their miseries, and made the Muses, Apollo their leader, and Dionysus their fellow banqueters in the feasts of the gods that *men might be corrected*." He then goes on to trace the origin of *mousikê* and the dance to a divine gift, the sense of order and rhythm.

affects people who lose control of their emotions. You and I, as philosophers, will remain unaffected. At least I do; I'm not so sure about you!" For we note with some dismay that the catharsis is here mainly intended for "mechanics, general laborers," and such. One almost expects the usual phrase, "because of the depravity of our audiences." [16]

Aristotle also discusses the educational use of *mousikê* and considers at some length which musical modes should be used for educational purposes (ch. 6).

The *Poetics* must be read with the above chapters of the *Politics* in mind, not only in order to understand the meaning of catharsis, but because of the "moral" and utilitarian conception of the function of *mousikê* which these chapters express.

II

THE POETICS

The question is sometimes raised whether we should look upon the *Poetics* as a handbook of rules telling tragic poets how they should proceed in order to write good tragedies, or

---

[16] Even here the catharsis is perhaps not *entirely* restricted to unbalanced people in so far as "an emotion which strongly affects some is present in all to a moderate degree," and these may be more mildly purged. The full effect, however, is on the more unbalanced. There is no such restriction in the *Poetics*, where it does seem to apply to all. In this connection it may be remembered that the "melancholic" temperament, i.e., that caused by an excess of black bile, included in Peripatetic physiology "men distinguished in philosophy, politics, poetry and the arts." See *Problem* 30, and Croissant (note 13), pp. 79-80, 98-99. Nevertheless, the catharsis is still a purgation and is explicitly in the *Politics* restricted to the "recreational" function of *mousikê*. Tragedy's contribution to the life of leisure cannot have been catharsis, as the more balanced individual does not need it. For a full discussion of various interpretations of catharsis see I. Bywater, *Aristotle on the Art of Poetry* (Oxford, 1909), pp. 152-161. Gerald F. Else, in *Aristotle's Poetics, The Argument* (Harvard, 1957), pp. 224-32 and 423-47, makes the novel and interesting but not quite convincing suggestion that it is not the emotions of the audience that are "purified" but the tragic deeds themselves.

whether it is rather a collection of musings, often extraordinarily illuminating, by a great thinker on the subject of tragedy. It may, in part at least, have been intended to be the former; but there can be no doubt that its greatness is due to its being, in fact, the latter. The style is very uneven. Some parts are written with reasonable care, but other parts are abrupt, ill-constructed, repetitive, contradictory, even ungrammatical. More clearly than any other work of Aristotle, the *Poetics* can only have been a set of lecture notes with later additions and interpolations by the lecturer himself.[17] We may well envy the original audience who had the opportunity of asking a few questions for purposes of clarification!

Here we will briefly discuss some of the more important and controversial points. We will try to establish what Aristotle meant, not what he should have meant to satisfy our modern minds, nor what he should have said to avoid the ambiguity he so rightly deplored in others.

Art as Imitation

When Aristotle says that poetry is imitation he is following Plato, and he clarifies this rather ambiguous conception. In the third book of the *Republic* Plato used *mimêsis* in the sense, mainly, of impersonation;[18] in the tenth book he used it in a wider sense to mean emotional identification or *sympatheia* where he discusses the psychological effects of poetry, and also in the more natural sense of imitation when he argues that the poet who imitates sensual life (itself an imitation of the Ideal) is at two removes from the truth. In the *Laws,* however, Plato mentions the theory that art is

---

[17] It is fascinating to try to isolate such additions. The reader will find a thorough study of the *Poetics* from this point of view in D. De Montmollin, *La Poétique d'Aristote* (Neuchâtel, 1951), and Else's commentary.

[18] *Republic* 3. 392d and ff. See also 10. 595a-608d; especially 598b for the metaphysical sense, and 604e-605c for the psychological effect of *mimêsis*. Aristotle also uses the word once in the *Poetics* in the restricted sense of impersonation, where he says that, when speaking in his own person, a poet is not "imitating." See ch. 24, note 5 below.

imitation as an obvious truth accepted by poet, actor, and audience alike.[19] The same idea of art as "imitation" is found in Xenophon, and in Aristophanes as well.[20] This famous theory of imitation is, in fact, not a Platonic theory so much as a generally accepted view which Plato uses in differing senses for his own purposes in his attacks on the poets. Aristotle mentions it at the beginning of the Poetics, not as a view that has to be argued, but as one that can be taken for granted and made the basis for his argument that the different genres of poetry should be differentiated by the nature of their imitation, i.e., by differences in the objects, means, and manner of their imitation.

And indeed it *is* almost a truism (or at least it was until quite recently) that art must be true to life. This does not mean a photographic copy, although Plato deliberately reduces it almost to that meaning when he is arguing *ad poetam*. It means that the situations, characters, emotions portrayed or evoked (for to both Plato and Aristotle music is "imitative") must strike us as true, so that this recognition of the model in the imitation gives us the pleasure described in the fourth chapter of the Poetics. And Aristotle expresses all this by explaining that, if accused of untruth, the poet may reply that he is imitating things as they are, as they were, as they ought to be, or as men thought they were, i.e., that he is representing the present, the past, the ideal,[21] or men's beliefs about

[19] *Laws* 2. 668b-c: "Everybody would surely agree to this much about *mousiké*, that all its compositions are imitation and representation. Would not all men agree to this, the poets and the audience and the actors?"

[20] In Xenophon, *Memorabilia* 3. 10. 1-8, Socrates is proving to a painter that he can imitate or represent (ἐκμιμεῖσθαι) not only the physical, but the qualities of the soul as well. In Aristophanes, *Thesmaphoriazusae* 156, we find the notion of *mimésis* used humorously where Agathon is dressed as a woman to compose an ode for women.

[21] *Poetics* ch. 25. Not too much should be made of this "imitation of the ideal" as a new and peculiarly Aristotelian change in the theory of *mimésis*. It is found in Plato, *Republic* 5. 472d: "Do you think a man is any the less a good painter if he paints a model such as the most beautiful man would be, and, having made everything fit in this picture, then cannot prove that such a man can exist?"

them. But the converse of this is that he *must* represent one of these or else the critic is right. Aristotle does not allow mere fancy on the stage. *Mimêsis* has often been translated as "representation" and "to represent," but that misses the peculiar flavor of the Greek word, which *is* more restrictive. It also sidesteps an age-long controversy.

Evil on the Stage

Here again Aristotle is improving on Plato, who refused to allow any evil deed or person on the stage, all because of his fear of emotional identification on the part of the audience. Aristotle realizes that this in effect means no drama but at best a series of epic-like recitations with the occasional enactment of the "nicer" scenes. He accepts the ultimate moral purpose of tragedy when he states baldly that his characters must be "good," but he immediately qualifies this Platonic position when he gives as an example to be condemned the Menelaus in Euripides' *Orestes* because he is *"unnecessarily evil."* [22] In a later passage he states that, in judging whether a particular deed or speech is "good," we should look beyond the particular incident and relate it to the character, the circumstances, indeed the whole play. Looked at in this way, the particular evil deed or speech may be found "to secure a greater good or avoid a greater evil," i.e., it may serve the moral purpose of the drama as a whole. There is no evidence to support the contention that Aristotle's ultimate judgment on a drama as a whole is purely aesthetic—no Greek writer's appraisal ever was; such a divorce between the good and the beautiful is quite un-Greek—but he certainly takes a much more sensible and acceptable view of the matter than Plato did.

[22] In ch. 15. The later passage is in ch. 25. The use of καλῶς is here clearly moral (as so often), at least in part. The context makes this quite clear. It corresponds to Plato's use of εὖ in *Laws* 2. 669a-b.

A Good Action?

The same question of Aristotle's moral view of drama arises in connection with the first clause of his definition of tragedy: "an imitation of an action which is *good.*" Here the word is *spoudaios,* and those who want to empty it of moral implication translate "a serious action" or "an action of high importance." The action here is, of course, that of the whole play, not a particular incident. It is the commentators who create the problem by here again introducing the distinction between a moral and an aesthetic judgment which is foreign to Aristotle. He tells us himself a few lines later that an "action" derives its quality from the character and mind of the doer.

When the same word *spoudaios* is applied to a character, it is always in a context which we would call moral. However, Aristotle must use a fairly mild word, for characters who are completely virtuous or vicious are not, to him, fit subjects of tragedy (or of comedy either). It does not help us to speak of men "of a higher type," or "of a lower type" (*phauloteros*), for it would have sorely puzzled Aristotle, I believe, how a man could be of a higher type without being a better man, or of a lower type without being a worse one, and the nature of the action is tied to the nature of the man who performs it. To Aristotle, the *éthos* of a man included his mind as well as his morals, in fact his whole personality. Our word "character" has a much more restricted sense.

The definition of comedy provides an enlightening parallel. "Comedy is . . . an imitation of men who are 'inferior' but not altogether vicious. . . ." [23] There is no possible doubt of the

[23] At the beginning of ch. 5. Not only does Aristotle refer to the *Poetics* for a further explanation of catharsis (see above) but he also, in *Rhetoric* 1. 11. 29 (1372a 2), says that "the ridiculous has been sufficiently defined in the *Poetics*"; a similar passage, *Rhetoric* 3. 18 (1419b 6), states that the different types of jokes were also discussed in our treatise. It is supposed that a second book has been lost. Professor Lane-Cooper, in *An Aristotelian Theory of Comedy* (New York, 1922) has ingeniously recon-

moral significance of the word "vice" (*kakia*), and the inferior men have less of the same thing. This obviously carries over to the statement which follows a few lines later where tragedy is said to be the "imitation of *spoudaioteroi.*" We may translate this as "superior" or as "men of a higher type," but obviously to Aristotle (and I should have thought to any man of sense) a higher type of man is a "better" type of man! The same is true of the passage in the second chapter where Homer and Sophocles are contrasted with Aristophanes because they imitate "superior" men. Again (ch. 2): "Since those who make imitations represent men in action, these men must be either 'superior or inferior,' either 'better' (*beltious*) than we know them in life, or worse, or of the same kind. For character derives, one might say, from these qualities, and all men's characters differ in virtue (*aretê*) or vice (*kakia*)." The words in question are here so completely identified with words of clear moral significance that they simply cannot be emptied of moral implications when they are applied to characters, or to action (which derives its qualities from characters) anywhere in the *Poetics* in order to make Aristotle conform to the canons of judgment of modern commentators.

Aristotle fully realized that an art must be judged on its own premises ("correctness for a poet is not the same as for a politician"), but that these premises were, in the case of tragedy, purely aesthetic, and therefore amoral, is a thought that simply could not have occurred to him, and there are other passages of the *Poetics* to prove it.[24]

---

structed it. The evidence for a second book is carefully reviewed by A. P. McMahon in "A Lost Book of the Poetics," *Harvard Studies in Classical Philology*, 28 (1917), pp. 1-46. McMahon does not believe a second book was ever written.

[24] Other relevant passages are as follows:

In ch. 4 we are told that poetry developed in two directions "*according to men's character*. The more noble-minded imitated the noble (καλάς) deeds of noble men, the more common those of inferior men . . . ." This is, of course, the customary use of καλός in a moral at least as much as an aesthetic sense, and we are therefore not surprised to find the first

The Tragic Hero

Aristotle's remarks on the character of the tragic hero are among the most illuminating and suggestive in the book. They are extremely brief: he has just told us that the downfall of the virtuous man is not tragic; and neither is that of a complete scoundrel (ch. 13):

> We are left with a character in between the other two: a man who is not outstanding in righteousness, or in wickedness and vice, and he should fall into misfortune through some *hamartia*. He should also be famous, or prosperous, like Oedipus, Thyestes, and the noted men of such families.

And a few lines further, the best kind of plot requires an unhappy ending which must come about, not through wickedness, but "through a great *hamartia* in such a character as we have mentioned or one better rather than worse."

The requirement that the character be like ourselves makes possible the *sympatheia,* the emotional identification which is necessary if we are to feel pity or fear, for pity is defined in the *Rhetoric* (2. 8.) as:

> the kind of pain we feel at the sight of a fatal or painful evil which happens to one *who does not deserve it, an evil which we might expect to befall ourselves or one of those close to us* and when it seems near. Clearly, to feel pity a *person must think that he himself, or someone belonging to him, is liable to suffer* . . . .

---

type of literature imitating τὰ σπουδαῖα. In this context the word cannot be emptied of moral implications, however we translate it.

When we are told that poetry is σπουδαιότερον than history (ch. 9), we may translate this "a higher thing" or a more "serious pursuit" than history, but even here Aristotle means it is a *better* thing. It will be more beneficial in its result, make men better (morally and in every other way).

The word is also used in the passage discussed above (ch. 25), where Aristotle is correcting Plato's extreme rejection of evil on the stage: "We must not only look to see if the particular words or actions are good or bad (σπουδαῖον ἢ φαῦλον)" but keep in view the circumstances, the character, etc. Here, as far as I can see, *all translators take the words in the sense of morally good or bad,* for nothing else makes sense.

Aristotle, with typical Greek realism, recognizes that tragic pity can never be completely disinterested, and it seems reasonable that we should be able to identify ourselves more closely with a character who is neither hero nor villain.

There is an apparent contradiction, however, with the earlier statement (ch. 2) that the tragic character must be better than life (this was arrived at on other grounds, namely, that tragedy was "better" than comedy), and Aristotle seems conscious of this when he adds, a few lines later in ch. 13, "a character such as we have described or better rather than worse"; and again in the passage where he says the poet must imitate the portrait painter who draws a good likeness and yet makes it "more beautiful than life" (ch. 15). At any rate it must be sufficiently like life (i.e., like ourselves) for us to feel closely akin. Nor need we be disturbed by the next requirement, that the tragic heroes must be the great ones of the earth. Aristotle is no doubt thinking of the impressiveness of the tragic stage, and until very recent times the world's dramatists have largely followed his advice. In any case, the spectator will not find this "greatness" much of an obstacle to emotional identification in the dreamland of the theater.

Hamartia

The real problem in Aristotle's description of the tragic hero is the nature of *hamartia*. The word can mean mistake, error, flaw, wrongdoing, and it has been variously interpreted as "a moral flaw," "an error of judgment," or a mere "misstep."

Let us be clear, first, that Aristotle is describing the tragic character, and that the *hamartia* is in that character, not external to it, for then his actions would cease to be "probable or inevitable." It is quite possible for a man to be in such a situation that he is inevitably led into error through no fault of his own (Oedipus is a perfect example), where he is a victim of circumstances, but this merely begs the question, for it will still be the nature of his response to the circumstances that will both show his character and affect his tragedy. Aristotle does not say anywhere that the misfortune is his hero's fault, he only says that it comes about, in the play, through a *hamartia* in his character.

Granted then that the *hamartia* is in the character, is it a moral weakness or an error of judgment? Those who hold the first view believe that the hero is morally responsible for his tragedy; those who hold the second view seem to think that he is not. But are we not, here again, forcing upon Aristotle a choice between clear alternatives that are ours, not his? He does not say the hero is responsible for his tragedy or that it is his fault. All he says is that there is some flaw or weakness in the personality of the hero which brings about his tragedy. Indeed, this follows logically from his previous statement, for if the hero were flawless he would be quite perfect and no tragic hero. I do not believe that Aristotle here makes any distinction between a moral flaw and a flaw in mental judgment. Each is a flaw or weakness in the personality of the hero, either may bring about the tragedy or bring it about at that particular time; neither makes him deserve it, but either again may make it seem natural that it should come about and is therefore dramatically satisfying. Besides, if pity is to be aroused, the misfortune must be undeserved in any case. Aristotle is not concerned to fix any responsibility or blame but to see that the tragedy should seem "probable or inevitable."

This, I believe, is a good example of a seminal idea imperfectly realized and imperfectly expressed, but opening the way to such kindred notions as conflict within the personality, which is one possible kind of flaw—a lack of *sophrosyne* in the Platonic sense of integration and harmony.

Reversal and Recognition

Peripeteia or reversal (ch. 11) is *a reversal of direction or intent, not of fortune.* What is developing, or intended to develop, in one direction suddenly takes an unexpected and unintended turn. This implies many things, more than Aristotle could possibly realize; but to translate *peripeteia* by "the irony of Fate" or "the irony of events" is to falsify the thought and to destroy the simplicity of expression, the pointing straight to the root of things, which is one of the charms of the *Poetics*. True, it is often difficult to fit the simpler thought into our more complicated, and much vaguer, pattern of ideas.

So, too, with recognition. Here again Aristotle caught a glimpse of much more than he was able to formulate. It should be perfectly clear that he is thinking of recognition between persons, and all his examples are of that kind. This is completely obscured if we translate *anagnôrisis* by "discovery" or "disclosure." It is true that Aristotle himself realized that his idea was capable of much wider application when he added, almost as an afterthought: "There are, to be sure, other forms of recognition: the knowledge acquired may be of inanimate objects, indeed of anything; one may recognize that someone has, or has not, done something." But even this does not go far enough, and he immediately returns to the recognition of persons. The modern meaning of discovery is much wider, and if Aristotle had realized the implications of his own idea he would never have said that there is no recognition in the *Iliad* but that there is "throughout the *Odyssey*" (ch. 24). Every reader of the *Iliad* knows that the tragedy of Achilles comes when he "recognizes," after the death of Patroclus, that there are things in life more important than honor and personal revenge. It is a perfect example of discovery in the wider sense, but that wider sense cannot be found in Aristotle.

There are many other suggestive and illuminating ideas to be found in the *Poetics:* the overriding importance of the plot, the different types of tragedy, its six elements, the need for the poet to feel the emotions he tries to communicate, the right and wrong critical attitudes, the essential and incidental flaws, and so on. We may disagree with him, but he will often start a fruitful train of thought or a profitable discussion. His meaning, however, is in most cases clear.

III

RHETORIC AND STYLE

The influence of the *Poetics* upon European literature and criticism since the Renaissance can hardly be exaggerated, but the book seems to have been lost in antiquity and had little or no influence upon the ancient critics in the centuries following Aristotle's death. The opposite is true of the *Rhetoric;* it continued to be read by Aristotle's successors, and later critics were familiar with it. In particular, the discussion of style which constitutes the first twelve chapters of the third book set a pattern of objective criticism which was consistently followed from then on. If the influence of the *Rhetoric* on modern criticism is less direct, it is no less important, and it may well be said that, taken together, the *Poetics* and those chapters of the *Rhetoric* which are here also translated contain the essential thought of Aristotle on poetry and literature, in so far as it is extant.

The *Rhetoric* is very different from the *Poetics* in both manner and method, and it must be read against the background of the rhetorical studies which flourished in classical times, for Aristotle is here writing the kind of book which the more thoughtful rhetoricians might have written on their own subject had they been more philosophically minded; for the fifth- and fourth-century rhetoricians had, independently of the philosophers, developed a quite different approach to literature.

With the development of full democracy in the fifth century, which brought political power within the reach of those who could sway a jury or an assembly, there arose an urgent demand for training in the art of speaking. When Gorgias of Leontini visited Athens in 427 B.C. and brought with him from Sicily all the technical tricks of his rhetorical trade, he took the city by storm. It was he who first claimed for the art of expression in prose an equal place with poetry. He was ridiculed by Aristotle and later critics for his poetic diction, his farfetched metaphors, his word jingles, his too carefully balanced clauses and antitheses, but his immediate influence was very great and we can trace it in the whole development of Greek style through the late fifth and the fourth century. All the Sophists, different as they were, had this interest in language in common. Textbooks on argumentation, on the ways to rouse the emotions, on figures of speech and thought, abounded during the next century. These Plato, and later Aristotle, treated with some contempt, as indeed they strongly attacked the Sophists and rhetoricians for their moral irresponsibility, their complete indifference to truth and to moral values. The greatest immediate educational influence, however, lay not in the schools of philosophy but with the rhetoricians and in particular in the school of Isocrates.

This remarkable man, who during his long life (436-338 B.C.) taught most of the prominent citizens of Athens, was, it is true, more than a mere rhetorician, for he did take note of moral values and tried to instill in his pupils a general philosophy of life. However, he had nothing but contempt for what he termed "useless" knowledge. His educational theory was that one should learn to speak well on great subjects. To do this one must have a sound practical knowledge of the questions of the day, and in order to make a good impression upon an audience one also needed to be a good man.[25] Isocrates was a careful stylist; he never wrote an inelegant sentence; his avoidance of hiatus,[26] for example, was notorious. It should be added that a physical handicap prevented him from public speaking. His works are in the form of speeches, but *logos* for him means the written as well as the spoken word. He estab-

---

[25] See Isocrates, *Antidosis* 45-100; *Panathenaicus* 1-32; *Panegyricus* 1-31.

[26] Hiatus occurs where a word ends with a vowel and the next word begins with the same or another vowel. Isocrates notoriously avoided such clash of vowels.

lished "rhetoric" as *the* subject of higher education, and it is his kind of education which was to hold the field in Rome and was advocated by Cicero and Quintilian.

In contrast to Isocrates, we have one fourth-century example of the more purely rhetorical teaching in the *Rhetorica ad Alexandrum,* preserved among the works of Aristotle but definitely not written by him. It displays a completely cynical, amoral attitude, and is concerned only to show what particular arguments and rhetorical devices will be effective under particular circumstances. It is against the background of both Isocrates and books like the *Rhetorica* that Aristotle's own *Rhetoric* must be appreciated. In part it is an answer to Plato, for it maintains that rhetoric *is* a *technê,* an art or craft, and sets out the limited knowledge that is essential to it; in part it may be said to establish the Isocratean theory of education on a more solid philosophic base; in part it is a strong protest against the amoralism of the rhetorical technicians.

The Greek word *rhetorikê* has a much wider significance than our word "rhetoric." The desire to be able to speak in public had provided the original stimulus for the study of language, and "the orator" always remained, in classical times, *the* prose artist, just as for Aristotle the writer of tragedies was *the* poet. But the study of *rhetorikê* was conceived as the art of language, especially in prose. We should not forget that, in the *Poetics,* Aristotle himself refers us to the *Rhetoric* for the means by which to express thought even in verse. If the ancients rarely made a clear distinction between the written and the spoken word it was in part because the practice of silent reading was quite unknown. To read meant to read aloud (or to have a slave read to you), so that even the written word was always *heard.* This helps to explain the emphasis in ancient criticism upon the sound of words and the importance attached to prose rhythm.

We find in the section of the *Rhetoric* which treats of style a number of basic principles expressed for the first time in extant literature. Not all of them were original with Aristotle, but we may well doubt whether any of them had been so clearly stated before. Most of them became commonplaces at once, and many of them still are.

The method is completely a priori (as it is in the *Poetics*) and totally objective. Aristotle lays down rules and principles, he describes the different types of metaphors, etc., and then illustrates them by brief examples from prose and poetry: a happy phrase, a good metaphor, a satisfactory rhythmic clause, and the like. This method, in less able hands, when lists of figures or qualities of speech took the place of a thought-out and organic classification, developed into that rhetorical approach to literature which considers it a mere treasure house of successful rhetorical devices. The works of the later rhetoricians often sink to that level.

In the *Rhetoric,* as in the *Poetics,* Aristotle has his weaknesses and his prejudices. He never, for example, quotes from Demosthenes, probably because of his strong dislike of the orator's elaborate periods and of his almost excessive use of the inversion of the natural order of words and thought which is hyperbaton. Aristotle analyzes, classifies, and illustrates; his power of clear analysis leads him to set down some basic principles, in this case less controversial and less obscure, which lie at the root of good prose style as some of his more striking statements in the *Poetics* lie at the very root of successful tragedy.

G. M. A. GRUBE

SELECTED BIBLIOGRAPHY

General

Atkins, J. W. H., *Literary Criticism in Antiquity* (2 vols.; Cambridge, 1934, republished London, 1952).

Baldwin, C. S., *Ancient Rhetoric and Poetic Interpreted from Representative Works* (New York, 1924).

Denniston, J. D., *Greek Literary Criticism,* a collection of translations with a general introduction (New York, 1924).

Nahm, Milton C., *Aesthetic Experience and its Presuppositions* (New York, 1946).

Roberts, W. Rhys, *Greek Rhetoric and Literary Criticism* ("Our Debt to Greece and Rome Series" [London, 1928]).

Sikes, E. E., *The Greek View of Poetry* (London, 1931).

The Poetics

The chief editions and commentaries have been described in the Note on the Text, p. xxxii. Of these Bywater and Gudeman give a full commentary on all matters of detail as well as on more general questions. Butcher's work consists of the text and translation (as does Bywater's), followed in his case by a few substantial essays on various aspects of Aristotle's theory of poetry and the arts. Else takes up the text section by section, with translation of each, and discusses the problems as they arise; a full statement of the views of others, as well as his own, will be found at each point. Among the following, the brief books by Humphrey House and F. L. Lucas are especially useful to the general reader:

Cooper, Lane, *Aristotle on the Art of Poetry,* an amplified version with supplementary illustrations (Ithaca, 1947).

———, *An Aristotelian Theory of Comedy,* with an adaptation of the *Poetics* and a translation of the *Tractatus Coislinianus* (New York, 1922).

House, Humphrey, *Aristotle's Poetics,* revised with a preface by Colin Hardie (London, 1956).

Lucas, F. L., *Tragedy, Serious Drama in relation to Aristotle's Poetics,* revised and enlarged (London, 1957).

xxxi

The Rhetoric

Cope, E. M., *An Introduction to Aristotle's Rhetoric,* with analysis, notes, and appendices (London, 1867).

—— and Sandys, J. E., *The Rhetoric of Aristotle,* with a commentary (3 vols.; Cambridge, 1877).

Freese, J. H., *Aristotle, The Art of Rhetoric,* with an English translation (New York, 1926).

Roberts, W. Rhys, *Aristotle, Rhetorica,* in Vol. XI of the Oxford translation of Aristotle, ed. W. D. Ross (Oxford, 1924).

NOTE ON THE TEXT

The standard English editions of the *Poetics* are S. H. Butcher's *Aristotle's Theory of Poetry and the Fine Arts,* first published in 1895 (London, Macmillan) and Ingram Bywater's *Aristotle on The Art of Poetry* (Oxford, 1909). The other standard modern edition is A. Gudeman's *Aristotles περὶ ποιητικῆς* (Berlin, 1934). Gerald F. Else's massive commentary, *Aristotle's Poetics, The Argument* (Harvard, 1957), reached me only after my translation was in the printer's hands. It contains many novel interpretations of time-honored problems, and though I cannot accept his main conclusions, his full treatment of the problems has been both helpful and illuminating.

All four of the above works will be referred to in the notes by the author's name only.

I have generally followed Butcher's text, except that here and there I have translated a phrase which he marked by [ ] for deletion. Any other significant divergences from his text are indicated in the notes.

A biographical index has been added in order to help the reader identify Aristotle's frequent references to mythological figures, poets and their works.

G. M. A. G.

THE POETICS

THE POETICS

I

Our subject is the art of poetry in general and its different genres, the specific effect of each genre, the way to construct stories to make good poetry,[1] the number and nature of its constituent elements, and all other matters which belong to this particular inquiry. And let us begin as is natural, with basic principles.

Poetry as Imitation

The epic, tragedy, comedy, dithyrambic poetry,[2] most music on the flute and on the lyre—all these are, in principle, imitations.[3] They differ in three ways: they imitate different things, or imitate them by different means, or in a different manner.

Differences in Means of Imitation

Some people imitate and portray many things by means of color and shape (whether as conscious artists or through force of habit); others imitate by means of the voice. So all the arts we have mentioned produce their imitations by means of

[1] The word here is ποίησις, i.e., poetry, but from the very beginning Aristotle has tragedy in mind (for of course there is and was poetry without story or plot). This leads him here and elsewhere (e.g., the first sentence of ch. 2 and note 1) to make general statements about poetry which apply only to certain types of poetry, and to tragedy in particular. We should also note that the word translated "constituent elements" is μόρια, the word he later uses (ch. 6) to designate the six elements of tragedy: plot, character, thought, diction, music, and spectacle.

[2] The dithyramb was a choral song, originally in honor of Dionysus. In the sixth century it seems to have had a strict formal strophic structure, but by the middle of the fifth century its formal structure disappeared, in contrast to the lyrics of tragedy. Its prelude in particular was of no set length, and could almost become a separate poem.

[3] For the meaning of imitation in this context, see Introduction, pp. xviii-xx.

3

rhythm, speech, and melody, using them separately or together. For example, melody and rhythm are the two means used when playing the flute or the lyre, or other instruments which may have a similar effect, such as the pipes. The art of dancing uses rhythm only, without melody, yet its rhythmic patterns, too, imitate character, emotions, and actions.

No Greek Word for Literature

Now the art which imitates by means of words only, whether in prose or verse, whether in one meter or a mixture of meters, this art is without a name to this day. We have no common name which we could apply to the mimes [4] of Sophron or Xenarchus and the Socratic dialogues, and also to any imitations that may be written in iambics, elegiacs, or other such meters. It is true that people join the word poet to the meter and speak of elegiac poets or epic poets, but they give the same name to poets merely because they use the same meter, and not because of the nature of their imitation. The same name is applied even to a work of medicine or physics if written in verse; yet except for their meter, Homer and Empedocles have nothing in common: the first should be called a poet, the second rather a physicist. And if a man should mix all meters, as Chaeremon made his *Centaur* a metrical medley, we must call him also a poet. Distinctions should be made in the manner suggested above. [5]

Certain poetic compositions, such as dithyrambic and nomic poetry, [6] tragedy and comedy, use all the means mentioned: rhythm, music, and meter. They differ because some use them

1447 b (left margin)

4 The mime was a short sketch, often in rhythmical prose, representing scenes from daily life.

5 Aristotle means that different kinds of poetry should be distinguished not by the meter but by the nature of the imitation, i.e., what objects it imitates, by what means, and in what manner, as stated again in the next paragraph.

6 The *nómos* was a musical lyric associated with the name of Terpander (early seventh century). Its later forms were, like the dithyramb, without strophic structure.

all simultaneously while others use them in turn. These, then, are the differences between the arts, based on the means used in imitation.

II

Differences in Models of Imitation

Since those who make imitations represent men in action,[1] these men must be superior or inferior, either better than those we know in life, or worse, or of the same kind. For character is nearly always derived from these qualities and these only, and all men's characters differ in virtue and vice.[2] We can see this in painting: Polygnotus represented men as better than life, Pauson represented them as worse, and Dionysius made them like life. Obviously, these differences also occur in each of the kinds of imitation we have mentioned; they are different because they imitate different models in this way.

The same distinctions can exist in dancing, in the music of the flute or the lyre, and also in prose or in such poetry as is unaccompanied by music. Homer, for example, represents men better than those we know, Cleophon makes them like those we know in life, while Hegemon of Thasos, the first

1448 a

[1] Aristotle here again seems to be generalizing too far. He has not actually said that all poetry is imitation, but he has certainly implied it. He ignores lyric poetry throughout, but even the dithyramb or nome (which he has mentioned) need not always imitate "men in action" (cf. ch. 1, note 1), nor do the lyrics of tragedy.

He also explains the main difference between tragedy and comedy by a difference in the object imitated. This is largely true, but the same actions can be represented as heroic or ridiculous, and burlesques of epic story were frequent in fourth-century comedy. Aristotle is forcing the differences between different genres into the strait jacket of his three (and only three) possible bases of difference.

[2] Note that the difference between the objects of imitation is here clearly stated in moral terms: men's characters differ because of their good and bad qualities, κακίᾳ . . . καὶ ἀρετῇ. For the word σπουδαῖος, i.e., (morally) superior see Introduction, pp. xxi-xxii.

writer of parodies, and Nicochares, the author of the *Deiliad*,[3] make them worse. The same is true in dithyrambic and nomic poetry, for one might represent the Cyclops after the manner of Timotheus or that of Philoxenus. Tragedy and Comedy differ in the same way: tragedy imitates men who are better, comedy imitates men who are worse than we know them today.

III

Differences in Manner of Imitation

The third difference lies in the manner in which each of these things is imitated. One may imitate the same model by the same means, but do it in the manner of the narrator either in his own person throughout or by assuming other personalities as Homer does, or one may present the personages one is imitating as actually performing actions before the audience.[1]

There are, then, as we said at the beginning, these three differences in imitations: the difference of means, the difference of models, and the difference of manner. In one respect, Sophocles is the same kind of imitator as Homer, for both imitate superior men; in another aspect he is like Aristophanes, for both present their characters in action. That is why their works are called dramas, because they represent men "doing."

Dorian Claims

The Dorian claim to have originated both tragedy and comedy is based on similarities of words. Comedy is claimed

---

[3] The Greek word δειλός means a coward, so that a *Deiliad* is the epic of a poltroon.

[1] Aristotle means: (a) straight narrative without direct speech, (b) narrative varied by letting the characters speak in their own persons (three fifths of the *Iliad* is said to be in direct speech), and (c) dramatic presentations without narrative. Plato (*Republic*, 3.392d) is more exact: his terms are: simple narrative, impersonation (μίμησις), and a mixture of the two.

by the Megarians, both by those in Greece who say it had its origin when their democracy was established, and by those in Sicily because their poet Epicharmus was much earlier than Chionides and Magnes. Tragedy is also claimed by certain Peloponnesians. The Dorians say their neighboring villages are called *kômai* while the Athenians call theirs *demes,* and that "comedians" were so named, not from the word *komazein* (to revel), but because they were despised in the city and wandered out through the villages. Moreover, they say that they express action by the verb *dran*,[2] whereas the Athenians use *prattein.*

1448 b

So much for the number and nature of the differences found in imitations.

IV

The Origins of Poetry

In general, two causes,[1] both inherent in man's nature, seem to have led to the birth of poetry. Imitation is natural to man from childhood; he differs from the other animals in that he is the most imitative: the first things he learns come to him through imitation. Then, too, all men take pleasure in imitative representations. Actual experience gives proof of this: the sight of certain things gives us pain, but we enjoy looking at the most exact images of them, whether the forms of animals which we greatly despise or of corpses. The reason is that learning things is most enjoyable, not only for philosophers but for others equally, though they have but little experience of it. Hence they enjoy the sight of images because they learn as they look; they reason what each image is, that there, for example, is that man whom we know. If a man does not know

2 Hence the word *drama.*

1 At first sight Aristotle announces two causes and then gives four: (a) man is an imitative animal, (b) he takes pleasure in seeing imitations, (c) he likes to learn, and (d) melody and rhythm too are congenial. The confusion is only apparent, the first three are one: man is imitative. The last is a second and different reason: man's aptitude for melody and rhythm. For this aptitude as the origin of *mousikê* see Plato, *Laws* 2, 653e ff. Cp. for (b) *Rhet.* 1. 11. 23.

the original, the imitation as such gives him no pleasure; his pleasure is then derived from its workmanship, its color, or some similar reason.

Next, imitation and melody and rhythm are ours by nature (meter being clearly a part of rhythm); so men were naturally gifted from the beginning, and, progressing step by step, they created poetry out of their random utterances.

Poetry developed in different ways according to men's characters. The more serious-minded imitated the noble deeds of noble men; the more common imitated the actions of meaner men; the latter wrote satiric verse while the former wrote hymns and encomia. We cannot mention any satiric work before Homer, though there were probably many, but we can begin with his *Margites* 2 and other things of the kind. The iambic meter was introduced because it was particularly suitable to this type of poetry, and such a poem is called *iambeion* to this day, because men used to satirize each other in this meter.

The History of Tragedy

Some of the old poets wrote heroic, others wrote iambic verse. Homer was certainly the greatest writer of serious-minded poetry; he stands alone not only because he wrote well but also because he dramatized his imitations. He was also the first to exhibit the different forms of comedy, and he dramatized the laughable, but not the personal satire. His *Margites* bears the same relation to comedy as the *Iliad* and the *Odyssey* do to tragedy.

1449 a

2 The *Margites* was an old comic epic. One of the very few remaining fragments is the famous line quoted by Plato (?) in the *Second Alcibiades* (147b): "He knew many things, and all of them badly." The ascription to Homer is doubtful, as are many points in the short history of tragedy and comedy which follows, particularly the derivation of tragedy from "the leaders of the dithyramb"—where Aristotle means that the leader came forward with a "speech" between choral lyrics—and from the satyr play, i.e., the fourth and comic play which followed a tragic trilogy. Our only extant example is Euripides' *Cyclops*. See, however, S. M. Adams in *Phoenix*, IX (1955) 4, 170-74.

When tragedy and comedy were known, men were led by their own nature to one or the other; one type of man came to write comedies instead of lampoons, the other type produced tragedies instead of epics, because these later forms of poetry were more important and more highly esteemed than the earlier. It is not our purpose here to inquire whether or not tragedy is now fully developed in its various parts, or indeed whether it is to be judged in itself or in relation to its audience. That is another question.

Tragedy first arose without deliberate intent, as did comedy also. The former originated with the leaders of the dithyramb, the latter with the leaders of the phallic songs which even today remain customary in many cities. Tragedy developed little by little as men improved whatever part of it became distinct. Many changes were introduced into tragedy, but these ceased when it found its true nature.[3] Aeschylus was the first to introduce a second actor; he also made the chorus less important and gave first place to the spoken parts. Sophocles added both a third actor and painted scenery. It is only at a late date that short incidents and the language of ridicule developed in length and dignity as the satyr-play changed into tragedy. The iambic trimeter replaced the trochaic tetrameter which had been used at first because the poetry was then satyric[4] and more closely related to the dance.

When spoken parts came in, nature herself found the appropriate meter, as the iambic is of all meters most like ordinary speech. This is proved by the fact that iambic lines occur most frequently in ordinary conversation, whereas hexameters occur but rarely, and then only when we abandon

[3] There is an apparent contradiction here, since Aristotle has just told us that it is not to his present purpose to discuss whether tragedy "is now fully developed." It is, however, only apparent. Tragedy has, he considers, attained its essential form and nature, i.e., choral and spoken parts, and the six parts or elements to be developed in ch. 6. It may, however, not have attained its fullest development "in its various parts," i.e., within its essential form.

[4] Satyric poetry is that of the satyr-play previously mentioned, which usually had a chorus of satyrs, and has nothing to do with satire.

conversational cadences. As for the number of *epeisodia*[5] and the way the other features of tragedy are said to have been elaborated, let us consider these also to have been dealt with, for to discuss them one by one would surely be a lengthy task.

V

The History of Comedy

Comedy is, as we said, an imitation of men who are inferior but not altogether vicious. The ludicrous is a species of ugliness; it is a sort of flaw and ugliness which is not painful or injurious. An obvious example is the comic mask, ugly and twisted but not painful to look at.[1]

1449 b   We know how tragedy changed and who made the changes, but comedy was not seriously pursued at first and its development is obscure. Only in more recent times was comedy produced at public expense;[2] before that it was performed by

---

[5] An ἐπεισόδιον is any part of a tragedy which stands between two choral odes. We may translate it by "act" as the nearest equivalent.

[1] This definition of comedy is less complete than the definition of tragedy at the beginning of the next chapter, but is parallel as far as it goes. The inferiority of the comic character is obviously conceived in moral terms: αἶσχος connotes ugliness both physical and moral, and the ἁμάρτημα or flaw here also resides in the character (see Introduction, pp. xxi-xxv). Such a flaw may be moral, mental or even physical. Plato, in *Philebus* 48c-49c, suggests that a lack of self-knowledge is characteristic of the butt of comedy, but he adds that if the individual is too powerful he inspires not laughter but fear. Aristotle may well have had that passage in mind, and he would certainly have accepted the lack of self-knowledge as one kind of comic flaw. He then adds that it must not be painful or injurious, an idea not unlike Plato's.

[2] Literally: "Only in recent times did the archon grant a chorus to comic performers." Greek dramas, both comic and tragic, were performed at public festivals in the public theater. The main festival for comedies was the Lenaea or Festival of the Winepress in the month of Gamelion (January-February). The dramatists submitted their plays to the appropriate archon or magistrate in charge, who selected those to be performed and "granted a chorus" to them, which meant that both chorus and actors were rehearsed and equipped at public expense. After the performances, a board of ten judges, one from each tribe, chosen by lot from

volunteers, and its various forms had developed before the
time of those who are called comic writers and are remembered. We do not know who introduced the masks, the pro-
logues, the several actors and the rest. Comic plots originated
in Sicily (Epicharmus and Phormis), while at Athens it was
Crates who first abandoned the lampoon to write comic works
with stories and plots of general interest.

Epic and Tragedy: Unity of Time

Epic poetry resembles tragedy in so far as it is an imitation
in verse of what is morally worthy; they differ in that the
epic has only one meter and is narrative in form. They also
differ in length, for tragedy tries to confine itself, as much as
possible, within one revolution of the sun or a little more,
whereas the time of an epic is unlimited. This, however, was
at first true also of tragedy.[3]

Some parts are common to both; others are peculiar to
tragedy. It follows that anyone who knows good tragedy from
bad also knows about the epic, as the elements of the epic are
present in tragedy, though not all the elements of tragedy are
to be found in the epic.

VI

The Definition of Tragedy

Epic poetry [1] and comedy will be discussed later. Let us now
take up the definition of tragedy which emerges from what

a list of names, selected the best play, or in the case of tragedies the best
tetralogy, and awarded the prizes.

[3] The reader should note that this is the only reference in the *Poetics*
to the famous "unity of time." It is not a precept, and it does not occur
in the discussion of tragedy as such. Aristotle simply recognizes the fact
that "as far as possible" tragedy "tries" to restrict itself to one day,
tragedy, that is, as he knew it, and as compared with the epic. To unity
of place there is no reference at all. He does, as we shall see, insist on
unity of action. A more thorough comparison of epic and tragedy is
found in chapters 24 and 26, where see notes.

[1] Literally: "the poetry which imitates in hexameters." This means epic
poetry, and the periphrasis might be confusing in English.

has been said. Tragedy, then, is the imitation of a good action, which is complete and of a certain length, by means of language made pleasing for each part separately; it relies in its various elements not on narrative but on acting; through pity and fear it achieves the purgation (catharsis) of such emotions.[2]

By "language made pleasing" I mean language which has rhythm, melody, and music. By "separately for the parts" I mean that some parts use only meter while others also have music. And as it is through acting that the poets present their imitation, one first and necessary element of a tragedy is the arranging of the spectacle. Then come music and diction, for these are the means used in the imitation. By diction I mean the actual composition of the verses, while the effect of music is clear to all.

The Six Elements or Aspects of Tragedy

Since it is an action which is imitated, it is performed by persons who must have qualities of character and mind, and from them we transfer these predicates to the actions also. Character and thought are the two natural causes of action; through actions men succeed or fail. The imitation of the action

1450 a

2 Some of the problems raised by this famous definition are discussed in the Introduction: for "a good action" see pp. xxi-xxii; and on the nature of catharsis pp. xv-xvii. My translation punctuates after χωρὶς ἑκάστῳ τῶν εἰδῶν and takes ἐν τοῖς μορίοις with what follows, so as to give the word μόριον the same meaning as in the following explanatory sentence. For a full discussion of this see "A Note on Aristotle's Definition of Tragedy" in *Phoenix*, XII (1958), 26-30.

After some hesitation, I have translated φόβος by "fear" rather than by "terror." It is true that the original Homeric meaning was panic or rout, and that *deos* is the milder word, but by the fourth century *phobos* was by far the most common word to indicate every kind of fear, while our own word "terror" seems to indicate a very violent, rather sudden, and often short-lived emotion, and its derivatives "terrify" and "terrifying" are not very appropriate. The exact meaning of *phobos* lies probably somewhere between fear and terror. See W. Schadewaldt's "Furcht und Mitleid" in *Hermes* LXXXIII (1955), 129-71.

is the plot, for this is what I mean by plot, namely, the arrangement of the incidents. Character, on the other hand, is that which leads us to attribute certain qualities to the persons who act. Thought is present in all they say to prove a point or to express an opinion. Every tragedy, therefore, has these six necessary elements which make it what it is: plot, character, diction, thought, spectacle, and music. Two of these elements are the means of imitation, one is the manner, three belong to the objects imitated,[3] and besides these there are no others. We may say that most poets use these elements; every tragedy, in much the same manner, has spectacle, character, plot, diction, music, and thought.[4]

Plot and Character

The most important of these is the arrangement of incidents, for tragedy is an imitation, not of men but of action and life, of happiness and misfortune. These are to be found in action, and the goal of life is a certain kind of activity, not a quality. Men are what they are because of their characters, but it is in action that they find happiness or the reverse. The purpose of action on the stage is not to imitate character, but

[3] Clearly, music and diction (language) are the means of imitation; the three elements which belong to the model are the plot, character, and thought. This leaves spectacle as belonging to the manner of imitation. This is different from the manner of imitation as defined in the first chapter, where the manner lies in its being either narrative or dramatic presentation (see ch. 4, note 2). The contradiction is, however, more verbal than real, for the dramatic presentation involves, indeed in a sense is, the spectacle, and the close connection between the two has just been emphasized.

[4] I follow Bywater in keeping the MS reading οὐκ ὀλίγοι αὐτῶν which Butcher and others delete and replace by πάντες in order to avoid the contradiction: Aristotle first says that most (lit., "not a few") poets make use of all six elements, and then adds that every play contains them. But the contradiction is only verbal. Every play contains all the elements of tragedy to some extent, but for the poet to make real use of them is a different thing. It is in this sense that we are told immediately afterward that a tragedy without character is possible.

character is a by-product of the action. It follows that the incidents and the plot are the end which tragedy has in view, and the end is in all things the most important. Without action there could be no tragedy, whereas a tragedy without characterization is possible.

The tragedies of most of our recent poets have no characterization and, generally speaking, there are many such poets. This is the difference, among painters, between Zeuxis and Polygnotus, for Polygnotus expresses character very well, while Zeuxis does not express it at all. Moreover, a series of speeches expressing character, well written and well thought-out though they might be, would not fulfill the essential function of a tragedy; this would be better achieved by a play which had a plot and structure of incidents, even though deficient in respect to character. Besides, the most important means by which a tragedy stirs the emotions reside in the plot, namely Reversals and Recognitions. Another argument is that those who begin to write poetry attain mastery in diction and characterization before they attain it in plot structure. Nearly all our early poets are examples of this.

The plot is the first essential and the soul of a tragedy; character comes second. Pretty much the same is true of painting: the most beautiful colors, laid on at random, give less pleasure than a black-and-white drawing.[5] It is the action which is the object of the imitation; the individual characters are subsidiary to it.

1450 b

Thought and Character

Thought is the third element in tragedy. It is the capacity to express what is involved in, or suitable to, a situation. In prose this is the function of statesmanship and rhetoric. Earlier writers made their characters speak like statesmen; our contemporaries make them speak like rhetoricians. A person's character makes clear what course of action he will choose or

5 Aristotle means that it is the pattern of colors which makes the picture, and so the pattern or structure of incidents, which is the plot, makes the tragedy.

reject where this is not clear.[6] Speeches, therefore, which do
not make this choice clear, or in which the speaker does not
choose or reject any course of action at all, do not express
character. Thought comes in where something is proved or
disproved, or where some general opinion is expressed.

Diction, Music, Spectacle

Diction is the fourth of the elements we mentioned. By
diction I mean, as I said before, the use of words to express
one's meaning. Its function is the same in verse and prose. Of
the remaining elements, music is most important among the
features of tragedy which give pleasure. As for the spectacle, it
stirs the emotions, but it is less a matter of art than the others,
and has least to do with poetry, for a tragedy can achieve its
effect even apart from the performance and the actors. Indeed,
spectacular effects belong to the craft of the property man
rather than to that of the poet.[7]

VII

Plot: Beginning, Middle, and End

Having now defined these elements, our next point is what
the plot structure should be, as this is the first and most im-

[6] With Bywater I have kept the words ἐν οἷς οὐκ ἔστι δῆλον: "where his
course of action is not clear." Aristotle uses ἦθος in a restricted sense: for
him character is expressed only where a course of action is decided;
where the factors involved in a situation are made clear or an opinion
expressed we have not character but thought. This distinction is highly
artificial, for the same scene, even the same speech, will often express both,
and at the same time. A choral ode, on the other hand, will express
thought but not character, since they make no "choice"—though even
here there may be exceptions.

[7] It is uncertain whether σκευόποιος means costumer (Bywater) or
stage carpenter (Butcher's "stage machinist"). Else (p. 278) rightly reminds
us that the ancient stage set was very simple, and he believes the reference
to be to the costumes. But Aristotle is obviously thinking of all the
"visual manifestations" (Else's phrase p. 280) of the performance and
σκευόποιος is probably used in a broad sense. The best modern equivalent
is probably "the producer."

portant part of a tragedy. We have established that a tragedy is the imitation of an action which is whole and complete, and also of a certain length, for a thing can be whole without being of any particular size. "Whole" means having a beginning, a middle, and an end. The beginning, while not necessarily following something else, is, by definition, followed by something else. The end, on the contrary, follows something else by definition, either always or in most cases, but nothing else comes after it. The middle both itself follows something else and is followed by something else. To construct a good plot, one must neither begin nor end haphazardly but make a proper use of these three parts.[1]

Size or Length

However, an animal, or indeed anything which has parts, must, to be beautiful, not only have these parts in the right order but must also be of a definite size. Beauty is a matter of size and order. An extraordinarily small animal would not be beautiful, nor an extraordinarily large one. Our view of the first is confused because it occupies only an all but imperceptible time, while we cannot view the second all at once, so that the unity of the whole would escape us if, for example, it were a thousand miles long. It follows that, as bodies and animals must have a size that can easily be perceived as a whole, so plots must have a length which can easily be remembered. However, the limit set to length by the circumstances of the dramatic presentation or by the perceptive capacity of the audience is not a matter of dramatic art. If a hundred tragedies were competing at once, the poets would compete with their eye on the water clock, and this they say happened at one time. What is a matter of art is the limit set by the very nature of the action, namely, that the longer is always the more beautiful, provided that the unity of the whole is clearly

1451 a

---

1 Aristotle is here expressing an important point in the simplest possible terms, that the plot should be *one* story and the whole story, and the beginning, middle, and end be such as to secure this unity of plot. This is essential to a good tragedy.

perceived. A simple and sufficient definition is: such length as
will allow a sequence of events to result in a change from bad
to good fortune or from good fortune to bad in accordance
with what is probable or inevitable.[2]

VIII

Unity of Plot

A story does not achieve unity, as some people think,
merely by being about one person. Many things, indeed an
infinite number of things, happen to the same individual,
some of which have no unity at all. In the same way one
individual performs many actions which do not combine into
one action. It seems, then, that all those poets who wrote a
Heracleid, a *Theseid,* and the like, were in error, for they
believed that, because Heracles is one person, a story about
him cannot avoid having unity. Now Homer, outstanding as
he is in other respects also, seems to have perceived this
clearly, whether as a conscious artist or by instinct. He did not
include in the *Odyssey* all that happened to Odysseus—for
example, his being wounded on Parnassus or his feigning
madness when the troops were being levied—because no thread
of probability or necessity linked those events. He built his
plot around the one action which we call the *Odyssey;* and
the same is true of the *Iliad.* As in other kinds of imitative art
each imitation must have one object, so with the plot: since it
is the imitation of an action, this must be one action and the
whole of it; the various incidents must be so constructed that,
if any part is displaced or deleted, the whole plot is disturbed
and dislocated. For if any part can be inserted or omitted
without manifest alteration, it is no true part of the whole.

---

[2] Aristotle's word ἀναγκαῖον refers to something that needs must happen and cannot be avoided. "Probable or necessary" is the usual translation, but the adjective "inevitable" is more natural, though "necessity"
may be the better noun.

IX

Tragedy and History [1]

It also follows from what has been said that it is not the poet's business to relate actual events, but such things as might or could happen in accordance with probability or necessity. A poet differs from a historian, not because one writes verse and the other prose (the work of Herodotus could be put into verse, but it would still remain a history, whether in verse or prose), but because the historian relates what happened, the poet what might happen. That is why poetry is more akin to philosophy and is a better thing than history; poetry deals with general truths, history with specific events. The latter are, for example, what Alcibiades did or suffered, while general truths are the kind of thing which a certain type of person would probably or inevitably do or say. Poetry aims to do this by its choice of names; this is clearly seen in comedy, for when the writers of comedy have constructed their plots in accordance with probability, they give their characters typical names, nor are they, like the writers of iambic lampoons,[2] concerned with a particular individual.

Names of Characters: Traditional Legends

The tragedians cling to the names of historical persons. The reason is that what is possible is convincing, and we are

1451 b

1 This brief reference to history is very unsatisfying and surprising from one who knew the works of both Herodotus and Thucydides. Aristotle fails to make any distinction between history and chronicle. His main point, that the first duty of the historian is to tell the facts, is, however, sound. When Aristotle is in a debating mood he is often unfair. Perhaps he was consciously rebuking the historians of the school of Isocrates for whom history was a form of rhetoric and who certainly had little respect for facts. See also ch. 23.

2 The lampoon is an attack on a particular individual. Comedy, as we saw in ch. 5, is a higher form of art because it has a plot—i.e., a story. The new comedy of the fourth century had elaborate plots and dealt very

apt to distrust what has not yet happened as not possible, whereas what has happened is obviously possible, else it could not have happened. However, there are tragedies which use only one or two of the well-known names, the others being fictitious; indeed a few tragedies have no well-known names at all, the *Antheus* of Agathon for example. Both the names and the events of that play are fictitious, yet it is enjoyable nonetheless. It is not, therefore, absolutely necessary to cling to the traditional stories which are the usual subjects of tragedy. In fact, it is absurd to strive to do so, for even the familiar stories are familiar only to a few, yet are enjoyed by all.[3] All this shows that it is the plot, rather than the verse, which makes a (tragic) poet, for he is a poet in virtue of his imitation, and he imitates actions. He is no less a poet if he happens to tell a true story, for nothing prevents some actual events from being probable or possible, and it is this probability or possibility that makes the (tragic) poet.[4]

---

much with types—the parasite, the clever slave, the miser, the young scapegrace, etc., and the names often betray this. The great names of legend: Achilles, Odysseus, Penelope, etc., (whom Aristotle calls "historical characters") had, through usage, become, in much the same way, types of the violent-tempered young man, the clever and brave rogue, the faithful wife, etc., and Aristotle considers them as such. That a great poet can make such "types" into individuals as well Aristotle does not mention, and probably did not grasp.

3 This statement is worth noting, for we are apt to assume that a Greek audience was familiar with the story dramatized. It is plain that, in the fourth century at least, this was much less true than our textbooks would have us believe.

4 Aristotle told us at the beginning of this chapter that actual historical events are not necessarily a unity; but certain actual events may be, and it is the business of the poet, when telling a true story, to select those events that are so connected in constructing his plot; which to Aristotle is the chief function of the tragedian. This is what he meant by "the way to construct stories to make good poetry" at the beginning of ch. 1.

Types of Plots

The episodic [5] are the worst of all plots and actions; and by an episodic plot I mean one in which the episodes have no probable or inevitable connection. Poor poets compose such plots through lack of talent, good poets do it to please the actors. As they write in competition and stretch the plot too far, they are thereby compelled to distort the sequence of events.[6]

1452 a

The object of the imitation is not only a complete action but such things as stir up pity and fear, and this is best achieved when the events are unexpectedly interconnected. This, more than what happens accidentally and by chance, will arouse wonder. Even chance events arouse most wonder when they have the appearance of purpose, as in the story of the man who was responsible for the death of Mitys and was watching a festival at Argos when the statue of his victim fell upon him and killed him. Things like that do not seem to happen without purpose, and plots of this kind are necessarily better.

X

Simple and Complex Plots

Some plots are simple, others are complex, just as the actions which they imitate are clearly one or the other. I call simple an action which is one and continuous, as defined above, and in the course of which the change of fortune

[5] The noun ἐπεισόδιον simply means any part of the action between choral odes (ch. 4, note 5) and is never used in a pejorative sense, but the adjective ἐπεισοδιώδης applied to the plot means episodic in our sense. See G. Norwood in *Classical Philology*, XXV (1930), 217-29.

[6] Aristotle seems to have two things in mind: a dramatist may stretch out a plot beyond its proper length to "pad" his work to the full length of a play, and this is a sign of incompetence; or even a good poet may write a scene with the special capacities of a famous actor rather than the requirements of his plot in mind.

occurs without recognition or reversal. A complex action is one wherein the change of fortune is accompanied either by recognition or reversal, or by both. These must emerge from the plot structure itself so that they are connected with what has gone before as the inevitable or probable outcome. It makes all the difference whether one incident is caused by another or merely follows it.

XI

Reversals and Recognitions

Reversal (*peripeteia*) is a change of the situation into its opposite, and this too must accord with the probable or the inevitable.[1] So in the *Oedipus* the man comes to cheer Oedipus and to rid him of his fear concerning his mother; then, by showing him who he is, he does the opposite; also in the *Lynceus* the hero is brought in to die and Danaus follows, intending to kill him, but in the event it is Danaus who dies and the other who is saved.

Recognition (*anagnorisis*), as the name implies, is a change from ignorance to knowledge of a bond of love or hate[2]

[1] Peripety or reversal should not be confused with the change of fortune which Aristotle calls μετάβασις. The metabasis refers to this change only, from bad fortune to good or, and this Aristotle considered better, from good fortune to bad (see ch. 14), and it involves no more than this change. Reversal, on the other hand, means that a situation that seems to or is intended to develop in one direction suddenly develops in the reverse direction (Introduction, pp. xxv f.). In *Oedipus King*, a messenger brings news that the king of Corinth is dead. Hearing that Oedipus had left Corinth because of an oracle which foretold he would kill his father and marry his mother, the messenger seeks to rid him of this fear by showing that he is not the son of the Corinthian king. But instead of relief, this disclosure leads to the revelation that Laius (whom he killed) was his father and, ultimately, that Iocasta is his mother and that the oracle is fulfilled. The *Lynceus* is attributed to Theodectes, but is unknown to us.

[2] Else (pp. 349-50) has rightly pointed out that in the expression εἰς φιλίαν ἢ εἰς ἔχθραν the word φιλία is used in the same special sense as in ch. 14, i.e., "not 'friendship' or 'love' or any other feeling, but *the objective state of being φίλοι, 'dear ones,' by virtue of blood ties*." It is

between persons who are destined for good fortune or the reverse. The finest kind of recognition is accompanied by simultaneous reversals, as in the *Oedipus*. There are, to be sure, other forms of recognition: the knowledge acquired may be of inanimate objects, indeed of anything; one may recognize that someone has, or has not, done something.[3] But the recognition which is most fully part of the plot and of the action is the kind we noted first. This kind of recognition and reversal will evoke pity or fear. Tragedy is the imitation of such actions, and good or ill fortune results from them.

1452 b

This recognition is between persons. Sometimes the identity of one person is known, and then only one person is recognized by the other; at other times both have to be recognized, as when Iphigenia is recognized by Orestes as soon as she sends the letter, but another recognition scene is necessary for her to recognize Orestes.

These things, reversal and recognition, are two parts of the plot. A third is suffering. We have discussed two of the three, namely reversal and recognition. Suffering (*pathos*) is a fatal or painful action like death on the stage, violent physical pain, wounds, and everything of that kind.

---

not that one person suddenly discovers that he loves another, but that the other is someone he should naturally love as being his father, brother, sister, etc. ἔχθρα is less specific, but presumably the opposite, namely, that someone thought to be "a dear one" turns out to be an enemy. This is added because Aristotle always fills in the logical alternatives, but it rarely happens in tragedy since it is the revelation of the bond of kinship which makes the tragedy. Else suggests that Jason's recognition, in the *Medea*, that his wife hates him is a possible example of recognition εἰς ἔχθραν.

[3] Aristotle here extends the meaning of recognition to include any kind of discovery or disclosure, but the discussion shows that he has the recognition of persons almost exclusively in mind (Introduction, p. xxvi). Recognition is therefore the best translation. In Euripides' *Iphigenia in Tauris*, Iphigenia promises to save the life of one of the two strangers (Orestes and Pylades) if he will take a letter to her brother Orestes, and thus reveals herself. Orestes then tries to convince her he is indeed her brother. The second recognition is not rated as high by Aristotle because it does not arise from the action to the same extent.

XII

The Sections of a Tragedy

We have previously mentioned the parts of tragedy in the sense of its qualitative parts. The quantitative sections, on the other hand, into which a tragedy is divided are the following: *prologos, epeisodion, exodos,* and the choral part, itself subdivided into *parodos* and *stasima.* These occur in all tragedies; there may also be actors' songs and *kommoi.*

The *prologos* is that whole section which precedes the entrance of the chorus; the *epeisodion* is a whole section between complete choral odes; the *exodos* is that whole section of a tragedy which is not followed by a choral ode. In the choral part, the entrance song (*parodos*) is the first complete statement of the chorus, a *stasimon* is a song of the chorus without anapaests or trochees; [1] a *kommos* is a dirge in which actors and chorus join.

We spoke previously of the parts which must be considered as qualitative elements of tragedy; these are the quantitative parts.

XIII

Possible Changes of Fortune

We must discuss next what a writer should aim at and what he should avoid in constructing his plot, how tragedy will come to fulfill its proper function. As already stated, the plot of the finest tragedies must not be simple but complex; [1] it

---

[1] Trochees ($- \cup$) and anapaests ($\cup\cup -$) are certainly more typical of the *parodos*, which the chorus spoke as they entered, than of the *stasima,* the odes which they sang when in position throughout the play. There are some exceptions, and the stasimon in *Medea* 1081-1115 is wholly anapaestic. This, however, is very unusual. It has been suggested that Aristotle is largely thinking of fourth-century tragedy. The authenticity of this whole chapter has been doubted, but without good reason.

[1] Simple and complex plots were explained in ch. 10: the latter have reversal and recognition.

must also represent what is fearful or pitiful, as this is characteristic of tragic imitation. It clearly follows that, in the first
place, good men must not be seen suffering a change from
prosperity to misfortune; this is not fearful or pitiful but
shocking. Nor must the wicked pass from misfortune to
prosperity; this, of all things, is the least tragic; nothing happens as it should, it is neither humane nor fearful nor pitiful.
1453 a A thoroughly wicked man must not pass from prosperity to
misfortune either; such a plot may satisfy our feeling of
humanity, but it does not arouse pity or fear. We feel pity for
a man who does not deserve his misfortune; we fear for someone like ourselves; neither feeling is here involved.

The Tragic Character

We are left with a character in between the other two; a
man who is neither outstanding in virtue and righteousness,
nor is it through wickedness and vice that he falls into misfortune, but through some flaw.[2] He should also be famous or
prosperous, like Oedipus, Thyestes, and the noted men of
such noble families.

The Best Plots

A good plot must consist of a single [3] and not, as some
people say, of a double story; the change of fortune should
not be from misfortune to prosperity but, on the contrary,
from prosperity to misfortune. This change should not be
caused by outright wickedness but by a serious flaw in a
character such as we have just described, or one better rather
than worse. This is proved by what has happened: at first
tragic poets related any kind of story, but now the best

[2] The "flaw" is a moral or intellectual weakness. See Introduction, pp.
xxiv-xxv, and ch. 5, note 1 above.

[3] This "single" plot is one story, a unity. It must not be confused with
the "simple" plot of ch. 10 (also referred to at the beginning of this
chapter) which is defined as being without reversal or recognition.
Aristotle unfortunately uses the same adjective, ἁπλοῦς, to describe both
kinds.

tragedies are constructed around the fortunes of a few families, and are concerned with Alcmaeon, Oedipus, Orestes, Meleager, Thyestes, Telephus, and any other such men who have endured or done terrible things. The best products of the tragic art have this kind of plot structure.

People are therefore mistaken when they criticize Euripides on this very point, because his tragedies are of this kind and many of them end unhappily, for this, as I said, is right. There is convincing proof of this: in the theater and in dramatic contests such dramas are seen to be the most tragic if they are well performed, and even though Euripides manages his plays badly in other respects, he obviously is the most tragic of the poets.[4]

The Double Plot of Comedy

The double plot, such as we find in the *Odyssey*, where, at the end, the good are rewarded and the bad punished, is thought by some to be the best, but in fact it holds only

[4] This praise of Euripides has usually been interpreted to refer only to the fact that many of Euripides' tragedies end unhappily. If, however, we look at this passage carefully, we see that Aristotle seems to mean a great deal more than that, and that Euripides is also praised for his type of tragic character at least. We have been discussing the tragic character; then, at the beginning of this section, Aristotle mentions *three* characteristics of a good tragedy: (i) it has a single plot (see previous note), (ii) it has an unhappy ending, and (iii) this ending is brought about by a serious flaw in the hero's character. He then says that experience confirms this and repeats that the best tragedies will have this kind of plot structure, which surely refers not only to the unhappy ending but to all three of the qualities mentioned, all of which concern the plot. We are then told that Euripides is wrongly criticized "for doing this in his plays" *and* because many of them end unhappily (if this referred to one and the same thing one would expect γάρ or the like, not καί). Surely this should mean that the plots of Euripides are of the kind described and have all three of the qualities mentioned above. To find Euripides praised for "single plots" surprises us, and it is possible that this first point is no longer present to Aristotle's mind, but it is quite unlikely that he is no longer thinking of the tragic character which is the main point in the whole discussion hitherto. I suggest therefore that Euripides is here praised for his type of characters *and* because his plays end unhappily. The

second place. It is the weakness of our audiences that places it first, and the poets seek to please the spectators.[5] The pleasure provided in this way, however, belongs to comedy rather than to tragedy; it is in comedy that those who, in the story, are the greatest enemies, like Orestes and Aegisthus, are reconciled in the end, walk off the stage as friends, and no one kills anybody.[6]

XIV

Pity and Fear should be due to Plot, not to Spectacle

1453 b   Fear and pity can be caused by the spectacle or by the plot structure itself. The latter way is better and argues a better poet. The story should be so constructed that the events make

---

"flaw" in most of Euripides' heroes and heroines is certainly not hard to find. It should also be noted that Sophocles is nowhere mentioned in connection with the flaw, for the mention of Oedipus (whose flaw critics have so laboriously sought for, and so unsuccessfully) above is in connection with a quite different point, that tragic characters should be the great ones of the earth.

What Aristotle has in mind when he goes on to criticize Euripides for not managing his plays well in other respects we can to some extent gather from other references in the *Poetics:* his Menelaus is unnecessarily evil, he makes excessive use of the supernatural (15), some of his recognitions do not arise out of the plot (16), he does not handle the chorus as well as Sophocles (see ch. 18, note 4), the arrival of Aegeus in the *Medea* is inexplicable, and Aristotle *seems* to be in sympathy with Sophocles' implied criticism of Euripidean realism (25). Surprisingly, Euripides is not criticized for lack of unity in some of his plots. See also *Rhetoric* 3, ch. 2, p. 69.

5 Weakness (ἀσθένεια) is a neutral word, but the sentiment is one of almost moral condemnation. Compare the remarks about "inferior audiences" at the beginning of ch. 26, and see Introduction, p. xi. In this case the audience is not cultured enough to prefer good tragedy.

6 Aristotle is of course quite right that a happy ending, the triumph of the hero over the villain, is not good tragedy, and the ancient critics always considered the *Odyssey* akin to comedy (see ch. 24, note 3). But why is it a double plot? Is it because the events in Ithaca and Telemachus' journey run parallel to the adventures of Odysseus himself? Only, I think, to the extent that it helps to bifurcate our attention at the end, which Aristotle has mainly in mind, for it is true that the triumph of virtue is

anyone who hears the story shudder and feel pity even without seeing the play. The story of Oedipus has this effect. To arouse pity and fear by means of the spectacle requires less art and a costly performance. And those plays which, by means of the spectacle, arouse not fear but only amazement have nothing in common with tragedy. We should not require from tragedy every kind of pleasure, but only its own peculiar kind.

The Tragic Situation

As the tragic poet must aim to produce by his imitation the kind of pleasure which results from fear and pity, he must do so through the plot. We must therefore investigate what sort of incidents are terrible or pitiful. Such actions must necessarily occur between people who are friends,[1] enemies, or neither. Between enemies neither the action itself nor the intention excites pity, except in so far as suffering is pitiful in itself. The same is true between people who are neither friends nor enemies. When, however, suffering is inflicted upon each other by people whose relationship implies affection, as when a brother kills, or intends to kill, his brother, a son his father, a mother her son, a son his mother, or some other such action takes place—those are the situations to look for.

Acting in Ignorance

It is not possible to undo the traditional stories, the murder of Clytemnestra by Orestes or that of Eriphyle by Alcmaeon,

---

both less tragic and less interesting, and that in those cases we are interested at least as much in the punishment of the villains. In a great tragedy, our interest is concentrated upon the hero (Oedipus, for example, or Hamlet, where the death of the king becomes almost incidental).

No one, certainly, could suggest that nobody kills anybody in the *Odyssey*. There is, however, no need to delete the last sentence (Else, pp. 399-406), for the sequence of thought is quite clear: a happy ending and double plot is not good tragedy; it is *more like* comedy; and in comedy the ending is not tragic at all, but the opposite.

[1] For the meaning of friends and enemies here see ch. 11, note 2.

but the poet must find ways to make good use of the given situation. Let us clarify what we mean by "good use." The deed can be done, as in the old poets, with full knowledge of the facts, as the Medea of Euripides kills her children. Or it can be done in ignorance of its terrible nature and this recognized later, as the Oedipus of Sophocles killed his father; this action, it is true, lies outside the drama, but it can happen in the course of a play, as with the Alcmaeon of Astydamas or with Telegonus in the *Wounded Odysseus*. There is still a third way: when someone who intends to do the deed is ignorant of the relationship but recognizes it before the deed is done. There is no further alternative, for one must act or not, either with knowledge or without it.

The worst of all these is to have full knowledge and intend to do the deed, and then not do it; this is not tragic but shocking, and there is no suffering; it is a type never or very rarely used, as when Haemon threatens his father Creon in the *Antigone*.[2] It is better to commit the crime. Better still is to do it in ignorance and to recognize the truth afterwards. Then there is nothing to shock, and the recognition is frightening. Best of all is the last alternative, the way of Merope in the *Cresphontes* where she intends to kill her son but does not do it when she recognizes him, or, as in the *Iphigenia*, where the sister is about to kill the brother, or in the *Helle*, where the son, about to give up his mother, recognizes her.[3]

1454 a

---

2 In the *Antigone* of Sophocles, King Creon condemns Antigone to death for ignoring his edict that her brother Polyneices, as a traitor, must not receive burial. Creon's son Haemon, betrothed to Antigone, threatens his father but does not carry out the threat. This alternative is not actually mentioned in the enumeration of the possible alternatives just concluded, though it is certainly implied. A statement of it may have dropped out of the text.

3 This conclusion is startling indeed. It seems to contradict the whole trend of the discussion of plot up to this point. If the recognition prevents the violent deed, we surely have a happy ending, which Aristotle emphatically declared, in the last chapter and elsewhere, to be inferior tragedy. It is the kind of play in which "no one kills anybody," which is

That is the reason why the subjects of tragedy are, as we said some time ago, provided by a few families. By chance rather than intent, poets found the way to provide these situations in their plots, and this forces them to go to those families which were thus afflicted.

We have now said enough about the arrangement of the incidents and the right kinds of plot.

XV

Four Aims in Characterization

In expressing character there are four things to aim at.[1] Of these the first and foremost is that the characters should be good. Words and action express character, as we stated, if they

---

closer to comedy. It is clearly less frightening or pitiful than, for instance, the *Oedipus*. No satisfactory explanation has been offered. Bywater suggests (note *ad loc.*): "The criterion which now determines the relative value of these possible situations is a moral one, their effect not on the emotions, but on the moral sensibility of the audience." But Aristotle's conclusion is the end of our search for pitiful and fearful situations; there is no hint of a change of criterion. Nor am I sure that Aristotle would agree to this subtle distinction between "emotions" and "moral sensibilities." Gudeman's stout denial of any contradiction, because Aristotle is here concerned not with plot structure but with the emotions, is even less convincing. See also Else, pp. 450-1.

[1] Aristotle's four requirements for the characters of tragedy are not as clear as they might be. The word translated "good" is χρηστός which, as applied to human beings, means morally good, i.e., virtuous. This meaning is then reinforced by linking character with choice (προαίρεσις, moral choice). Commentators here also, as with σπουδαῖος, try to empty the word of moral content by translating that the character must be "good of its kind," a meaning which the Greek word can bear when applied to things but not to people. However, the question is settled by Aristotle's own example. Menelaus in the *Orestes* is too *wicked*. Aristotle does, however, interpret "goodness" more widely than Plato did. (Introduction, p. xx.) The second requirement is that a character should be appropriate, i.e., true to type. Some commentators are shocked that Aristotle says a woman should not be brave (the Greek word ἀνδρεῖος, "manly," makes this easier) or clever, but the word δεινός might here mean "a clever

bring out a moral choice, and the character is good if the choice is right. This applies to every type: even a woman or a slave can be good, though the former of these is a weaker being and the slave is altogether inferior. In the second place, characters must be appropriate or true to type: there is a manly character, but it is not appropriate for a woman to be manly or a clever speaker. The third aim is to be true to life, and this is different from being good or true to type. The fourth is consistency. Even if the character represented displays inconsistency as a character trait, he must be consistent in his inconsistency.

Menelaus in the *Orestes* provides an example of a character which is unnecessarily evil; the lament of Odysseus in the *Scylla* and the speech of Melanippe are unsuitable and inappropriate; Iphigenia in *Iphigenia at Aulis* shows inconsistency: her supplication is quite unlike the character she displays later.[2]

In characterization as in plot structure, one must always aim at either what is probable or what is inevitable, so that a certain character will say or do certain things in a way that is probable or inevitable, and one incident will follow the other in the same way.

---

speaker," as Gudeman suggests. This would, as far as we know, suit the example of Melanippe. The third requirement is expressed by ὅμοιον, like, probably "like life," i.e., true to life (and so I have translated it) but it *might* mean "like their prototypes in legend," i.e., Achilles wrathful, etc., but as Aristotle regards these characters as historical this is ultimately the same thing.

Lastly, consistency. This is a good point excellently made: the need to be consistent in inconsistency is one of the striking phrases and thoughts in the *Poetics*.

2 The reference is to the *Orestes* of Euripides. We do not know the next two plays, but Melanippe presumably philosophized more than a woman should and it was unheroic for Odysseus to lament in the way he did. The *Iphigenia at Aulis* of Euripides represents the princess first horrified by, then glorying in, her sacrifice.

The Supernatural

The solution of the plot should also emerge from the story itself; it should not require the use of the supernatural, as it does in the *Medea* and in the threatened departure of the Greeks in the *Iliad*.[3] The supernatural should be used only in connection with events that lie outside the play itself, things that have happened long ago beyond the knowledge of men, or future events which need to be foretold and revealed, for we attribute to the gods the power of seeing all things. In the incidents of the play there should be nothing inexplicable or, if there is, it should be outside the actual play, as in the *Oedipus* of Sophocles.

1454 b

Characterization

Since tragedy is the imitation of characters better than those we know in life, we should imitate good portrait painters. They too render the characteristic appearance of their subject in a good likeness which is yet more beautiful than the original. So when the poet is imitating men who are given to anger, indolence, and other faults of character, he should represent them as they are, and yet make them worthy. As such an example of violent temper we have the Achilles of Agathon and Homer.[4]

[3] The Greek expression ἀπὸ μηχανῆς, translated "the supernatural," refers to the "machine" by which the gods were made to appear on the roof of the scene building, or to such similar devices as the "Chariot of the Sun" sent to save Medea in Euripides. Aristotle does not condemn the epiphanies of the gods, but would restrict them to revealing the past or future. In *Iliad* 2, Athena appears to stop a panic, and this must not be done in tragedy. The accusation that tragedians used the gods to get them out of difficulties is as old as Plato (*Cratylus* 425d) and was often made by the comic poets.

[4] The text is uncertain but the meaning seems clear. Homer's Achilles is a perfect example of the "flaw" which does not prevent nobility and greatness. Of Agathon's treatment of him we know nothing.

Care for Details of Presentation

These things the poet must keep in mind. Besides these, he must also pay attention to the visual and other impressions which, apart from its essential effects, a poetic presentation inevitably makes upon the audience, for frequent errors are possible here also. These are adequately dealt with in my published works.

XVI

Kinds of Recognition

What recognition is has already been stated. As to its different kinds, the first, least artistic but most frequently used through lack of talent, is recognition by tokens or signs. Some of these signs are congenital, like the spear-shaped birthmark of the Sons of Earth, or the stars which Carcinus used in his *Thyestes;* others are acquired, whether marks on the body like wounds, external possessions like necklaces, or the skiff which was the means of recognition in the *Tyro.* There is a better and a worse way of using these signs; both his old nurse and the swineherds recognize Odysseus by his scar, but the manner of their recognition is quite different. Recognitions deliberately brought about to prove one's identity are less artistic, as are all recognitions of this kind; but those that emerge from the circumstances of the reversal are better, as in the bath scene with Odysseus' old nurse.[1]

The second kind of recognition is that contrived by the poet; it is inartistic for this very reason, as Orestes in the

---

1 While Odysseus, still believed to be a beggar, is in his palace, his old nurse is told by Penelope to wash his feet (which is a natural proceeding arising out of the plot) and she recognizes the scar. This is the bath scene of *Odyssey* 19. Later, Odysseus, choosing his own time, makes himself known to Eumaeus and Philoetius and shows them the scar to convince them (*Od.* 21. 221-2). This does not emerge from the circumstances as naturally. For the *Iphigenia* see note 3, ch. 11. Of the other illustrations in this chapter we know besides the *Odyssey* only the *Choephori* of Aeschylus and the *Oedipus* of Sophocles.

Iphigenia brings about the recognition that he is Orestes. The recognition of Iphigenia follows from the letter, but Orestes says himself what the poet, not the plot, requires him to say. This is why it comes very close to the fault mentioned above in the case of Odysseus and the swineherds, for Orestes too could have had some tokens with him. The cry of the shuttle in the *Tyreus* of Sophocles also belongs here.

The third kind of recognition is through memory: we see one thing and recall another, as a character in the *Cyprians* of Dicaeogenes saw the picture and wept, or the recognition scene in the lay of Antinous, where Odysseus listens to the bard and weeps at his memories, and this leads to the recognition. 1455 a

Recognition of the fourth kind is by inference, as in the *Choephori:* someone like me has come, there is no one like me except Orestes, therefore Orestes has come. The same applies to Iphigenia in the work of the sophist Polyidus, for it was likely for Orestes to reflect that his sister was sacrificed and that the same thing was now happening to him, or for Tydeus in the play of Theodectes to say that he had come to find his son and was being killed himself. Similarly, in the *Phineidae,* the women, on seeing the place, reflected on their fate: that they were fated to die in this place from which they had been cast out.

There is a further kind of composite recognition based upon a wrong inference by one of the two parties involved, as in *Odysseus the False Messenger,* where one said he would know the bow he had never seen, and the other understood him to say he would recognize it, and thus made a false inference.

Of all these, the best recognition is that which emerges from the events themselves, where the amazement and the surprise are caused by probable means, as in the *Oedipus* of Sophocles and the *Iphigenia,* for it was probable that Iphigenia should wish to send a letter. This is the only kind of recognition which dispenses with contrived tokens and necklaces. The second best is recognition based on a correct inference.

XVII

Need to Visualize the Play

When a dramatist is constructing his plot and elaborating it by putting it into words, he must visualize the incidents as much as he can; he will then realize them vividly as if they were being enacted before his eyes, discover what fits the situation, and be most aware of possible inconsistencies. Let him be warned by the reproach made against Carcinus: in one of his plays no one who did not see the performance was aware that Amphiaraus was on his way up from the temple, but the play failed on the stage because the audience resented the inconsistency.

Emotions of the Dramatist

The poet should also, as far as possible, work out the positions and attitudes of the actors in the play. Given equal natural talent, those dramatists who are themselves emotionally affected are most convincing; one who is himself distressed distresses, one who is angry conveys anger most realistically. For this reason, a poet is either highly gifted or unbalanced; the unbalanced poet becomes one character after another, but the man of high gifts retains his critical sense.[1]

---

[1] That the writer (or speaker) must feel the emotions he is trying to arouse became a commonplace of the schools. See, e.g., Cicero, *De Oratore* 2, 45-6 (189-97) and Horace, *Ars Poet.* 99-108.

The text of the last sentence is uncertain. I have here translated the reading ἐξεταστικός, referring it to the man of talent. The usual reading, ἐκστατικός, means "beside himself" and is then taken to refer to the unbalanced poet (Aristotle calls him μανικός, mad), but it is not a proper antithesis to εὔπλαστος, which refers to something that can take on any shape, like clay. In any case, as Butcher (who adopts the usual reading) says, the contrast indicates that the talented poet is marked off from the unbalanced one "by a more conscious use of his critical faculty" (*Harvard Lectures on the Originality of Greece*, London, 1920, p. 147). See also his *Aristotle's Theory of Poetry and Fine Art*, p. 397, and Else, pp. 497-502.

We should note that this is the only passage in the *Poetics* which concerns itself with the feelings of the poet.

The Outline

In the process of writing, the dramatist must first lay out an outline of the story, even if he has invented it, and then fill it out with incidents. I mean that the outline should be considered as follows, to take the example of the *Iphigenia:* a girl who had been offered in sacrifice mysteriously disappeared; she was established as priestess in another country where the law required her to sacrifice strangers to the goddess; some time afterwards her brother arrived (the fact that the god for some reason had, by an oracle, instructed him to go there does not belong to the outline of the story, and the purpose of the oracle lies outside the plot altogether); on his arrival he is captured and is about to be sacrificed when he makes himself known, either in the manner of Euripides or in that of Polyidus who makes him say, as he naturally would, that not only his sister but himself were fated to be sacrificed. Hence he is saved. The next step is to assign the names and to fill in the incidents. The author must see to it that these incidents belong to his story, as in the case of Orestes, whose madness led to his capture, then to his being saved, since the victim had to be cleansed.[2]

The incidents of tragedy are short, while it is the incidents which give the epic its length. For the actual story of the *Odyssey* is not long: a man has been absent from home for

1455 b

---

[2] What Aristotle here has in mind is well explained by Else (pp. 505-6): the dramatist must keep the general outline of his plot in mind, in order to be sure that all the "episodes" or incidents are truly relevant so that his plot does not become "episodic." This naturally leads to a restatement of the difference between tragedy and epic in this regard.

In the *Iphigenia*, however, the escape itself is part of the outline, the manner of escape is a relevant "episode" (in the Greek sense, see ch. 9, note 5). So the madness of Orestes, though it does not belong to the outline, is a relevant "episode" because it leads to his capture and also helps to make the escape possible, for Iphigenia uses the need for cleansing the victim before sacrifice as a pretext to obtain a ship from the king, i.e., the means of escape. These and other "episodes" are Euripides' way of "filling in" the outline. They are of course essential to his play.

many years, alone and under the eye of Poseidon. The situation at home is that his possessions are being squandered by the suitors, and they plot against his son. He arrives home tempest-tossed; he makes himself known, attacks and kills his enemies, and is safe. That is the essential plot of the *Odyssey;* the rest is incidents.

XVIII

Involvement and Unraveling

Every tragedy consists of two parts, the involvement and the unraveling.[1] The incidents which precede the beginning of the play, and frequently some of the incidents within the play, make up the involvement, the rest is the unraveling. I mean that the involvement extends from the beginning to the part which immediately precedes the change to good or bad fortune, while the unraveling extends from where the change of fortune begins to the end. In the *Lynceus* of Theodectes, for example, the involvement includes what has previously taken place and the capture of the child, the unraveling extends from the accusation of murder to the end.

Four Types of Tragedy

There are four types of tragedy, the same number as the elements we mentioned earlier: the complex tragedy, in which reversal and recognition are the whole drama; the tragedy of suffering, like the plays on Ajax or Ixion; the tragedy of character, like the *Phthian Women* and the *Peleus;* and, fourth, the spectacular tragedy, like *The Daughters of Phorcys,* the *Prometheus,* and all the plays that are located in the

1456 a

---

1 The Greek terms are δέσις and λύσις, i.e., tying (e.g.) a knot, and untying it. The latter is more than the denouement (though this preserves the metaphor), and the former is more than "complication." It seems better not to use technical modern terms. The meaning of each is clearly explained, but the *Lynceus* is unknown to us. The text at the end of this section is uncertain but the meaning is clear enough.

Underworld.² One should try to achieve all four kinds or, if
not all, most of them and the most important, especially as
(tragic) poets are nowadays subjected to all kinds of unfair
criticism. Each type of tragedy has produced its good poets,

² There are three difficulties in this passage: (1) the parts or elements
of tragedy mentioned in ch. 6—plot, character, thought, diction, music,
and spectacle—were not four but six. The "complex" tragedy was not one
of them, and the two enumerations do not correspond. Gudeman in his
notes ingeniously suggests the reference to be to the same "parts" as we
find in ch. 24: "The different kinds of epic are the same as the kinds of
tragedy: it is either simple or complex, either an epic of character or of
suffering," and that an earlier and similar division into parts or elements
has been lost, but Aristotle says the *number* was the same, not that the
two divisions were the same. The "simple" tragedy must then be the
fourth member of our series (see below).

(2) The second type of tragedy is the παθητική. Now *pathos* can mean
passion or suffering; in fact the word combines the two meanings, but in
view of the explanation of *pathos* at the end of ch. 11, and of the examples given here, it is clear that Aristotle has the meaning of "suffering"
in mind. We do not know the plays referred to but any tragedy on the
madness of Ajax or the punishment of Ixion on his wheel in Hades is
likely to have stressed suffering. "Emotional tragedy" would therefore
seem to be a wrong translation.

(3) It is quite uncertain what the fourth kind of tragedy is, for the text
is corrupt. Bywater's reading of ὄψις, the spectacular, adopted in the text,
is the more generally accepted, though Butcher and Gudeman (see above)
read ἁπλῆ, simple. Again, the examples seem to make "the spectacular"
the more probable; tragedies set in the Underworld are likely to have
relied on spectacle.

Clearly, these types or aspects of tragedy are not mutually exclusive but
can and should be combined, as Aristotle immediately goes on to tell us.

It should be equally clear that he is here analyzing tragedy as he finds
it and not as he wants it, for *he has expressed disapproval of all these
types except the first.* The fourth, the spectacular, is clearly condemned at
the end of ch. 6. As for Butcher's reading of ἁπλῆ, the simple tragedy is
said to be inferior to the complex plot at the beginning of ch. 13. Else's
suggestion, ἐπεισοδιώδης (pp. 522-28), fares even worse, for the episodic
is the worst of all plots (ch. 9). The third type, the tragedy of suffering,
παθητική, fares no better, for mere πάθος is not really tragic, as we were
told in ch. 14: a dreadful deed inflicted upon an enemy does not excite
pity "except in so far as the suffering itself is pitiful"—πλὴν κατ᾿ αὐτὸ

but the same man is now expected to surpass all his predecessors in their own specialty.

It is with regard to the plot, more than anything else, that one is justified in calling one tragedy the same as another, that is, two tragedies that have the same involvement and unraveling. Many poets handle the involvement well but the unraveling badly. Both should be mastered.

Epic and Tragic Plots

It is necessary to remember what has already often been mentioned, and not to compose a tragedy with an epic plot structure, by which I mean a plot with many stories, as would be the case if someone were to make the whole story of the *Iliad* into a tragedy. In the *Iliad,* because of its magnitude, the different parts adopt a length appropriate to each, but in tragedies such length is contrary to the concept of the drama. One may prove this by referring to those who have made the whole story of the fall of Troy into a tragedy, and not, like Euripides, parts of that story only, or to those who wrote a tragedy on Niobe, but not in the way Aeschylus did. These writers have been hissed off the stage or at least been unsuccessful, for even Agathon was hissed off the stage for this reason alone.

Defective Plots

Yet in their handling of reversals and in simple plots these poets wonderfully achieve the effect they aim at, for indeed this sort of thing is tragic and satisfies our humane feelings,

---

τὸ πάθος. As for the second type, the tragedy of character, we remember that character is less important than plot and that you can have a tragedy without it (ch. 6).

This new classification then consists of Aristotle's idea of a good tragedy, the complex with reversal and recognition, and of three inferior types. When he goes on to say that one should use them all, I cannot help feeling that this is "because of the weakness of the audiences." Cp. what he says about style in *Rhet.* 3. 1 and note 5, ch. 13 above.

that is, when a clever but wicked man like Sisyphus is deceived, or a brave criminal is defeated.[3] This is probable in Agathon's sense when he said that many unlikely things are likely to happen.

The Chorus

The chorus must be considered to be one of the actors, an element in the play, and it should take part in the action not as in Euripides but as in Sophocles.[4] In later dramatists the songs are no more part of the story than of another tragedy, so that they are sung as interludes, a practice started by Agathon. Yet what difference is there between singing an interlude and inserting a speech or a whole scene from another play?

[3] Aristotle here deals with a number of defects which have not militated against a certain measure of success. Agathon failed on occasion because he had an epic plot. Others, successful in reversal and in *simple* plots (which we know are not the best), are tragic to some extent and satisfy our humane feelings ($\phi\iota\lambda\acute{a}\nu\theta\rho\omega\pi\sigma\nu$). This happens when a wicked person passes from prosperity to misfortune: "Such a plot may satisfy our feeling of humanity but it does not arouse pity or fear" (ch. 13). And Aristotle now goes on to illustrate these imperfect plots: a clever rascal is deceived, i.e., the change of fortune does not arise from any "flaw," as it would if he was not very clever. Nor does it when a brave but wicked man is defeated, as there is no lack of bravery. In both these cases bad men come to grief but this does not arouse pity or fear; moreover, the change is not due to any "flaw" in themselves. In this sentence I have followed Bywater who preserves the ms reading $\sigma\tau\sigma\chi\acute{a}\zeta\sigma\nu\tau\alpha\iota$ $\mathring{\omega}\nu$ $\beta\sigma\acute{u}\lambda\sigma\nu\tau\alpha\iota$.

[4] There is a double contrast here: (1) as against later dramatists whose choral odes were mere interludes (a practice started by Agathon) both Sophocles and Euripides treated the chorus as an actor; but (2) Aristotle prefers Sophocles' manner of doing this to that of Euripides, presumably because, though the choral odes still have relevance in the plays of Euripides, they are less obviously and directly relevant, as a general rule, than in Sophocles. On the chorus in Euripides see my *The Drama of Euripides* (London, 1941) pp. 99-126.

XIX

Thought

We have now discussed the other elements of tragedy, but diction and thought remain to be dealt with. Concerning thought, this should be dealt with in my treatise on rhetoric, for it belongs to that province of study. The expression of thought includes all the effects to be contrived by speech, and under this head come proof, refutation, the rousing of such emotions as pity, fear, anger, and the like, making things appear important or trifling. Now it is clear that in handling the incidents of a drama we must make use of the same rhetorical devices whenever it is necessary to make those incidents appear pitiful, fearful, important or probable, except for this difference: events on the stage are seen without our being told of them, whereas in a prose speech the events are expounded by the speaker and exist for the audience only through his speech. For what would be the function of an orator if the audience could get an impression of the events he deals with apart from his speech? [1]

1456 b

Diction: Modes of Expression

In matters of diction, one kind of inquiry deals with the modes of expression. The knowledge of these belongs to the art of delivery,[2] and to the person whose chief art this is: what,

1 Aristotle is here drawing a contrast between the orator and the tragic poet, and he expresses it as one between prose and verse because, as the tragedian is for him *the* poet, so the orator is *the* speaker and writer of prose. This contrast continues throughout the above passage; he does not draw a further contrast between "the speeches" and "the action" in tragedy, as most commentators interpret this passage. The audience in the theater see the events happening before them; the audience in a court of law have to rely upon the speaker to present them. It is true that messenger speeches also present and interpret events, but Aristotle nowhere distinguishes them from the rest of the action.

2 The distinction may seem forced, but by "what is a command" Aristotle means what is it on the stage, how does one utter and act it?

for example, is a command, a prayer, a statement, a threat, a question, an answer, or any other possible mode? No serious reproach is made against the poet for his knowledge or ignorance of these things. Would anyone agree with the criticism of Protagoras that Homer was at fault because what he thinks is a prayer is actually a command: "Sing, goddess, of the wrath"? The Sophist says that to order someone to do or not do something (the imperative) is in fact a command. We may therefore pass over this inquiry as belonging to another art than poetry.

XX

[This chapter is purely linguistic; it discusses what Aristotle calls the parts of speech or elements of diction: letters, syllables, connectives, nouns, verbs, statements, and defines each of them. It adds nothing to the study of criticism or poetry and its significance relates mainly to the Greek language only. The text is extremely obscure in parts. Its authenticity has been doubted, but without good reason. It may serve to remind us that the study of the elements of language had not been separated from the art of speech, whether in prose or verse. The chapter is here translated merely for the sake of completeness, and the reader may omit it and proceed to the next which deals with the *use* of words.]

Language as a whole consists of the following parts: the letter, the syllable, the connective, the noun, the verb, the article, the case, and the statement.

The letter is an indivisible sound; not every sound, however, is a letter, but only those which can combine to make a sound which has meaning. Even animals can utter indivisible sounds, but none of these I call a letter.

These letter sounds are vowels, semivowels, or mutes. A vowel sound is that which can be audible without anything being added to it; a semivowel is audible when another sound

---

He is obviously right that histrionics is not the art of poetry. The passage of Homer criticized by Protagoras is the first line of the *Iliad*.

is added,[1] like S or R; a mute has no sound of its own even when another letter is added, but in combination with another letter which has a sound of its own it becomes audible, e.g., G or D. These letter sounds differ in that the shape of the mouth varies in pronouncing them, also they are pronounced at a different place in the mouth, they are aspirated or not, they are long or short, their pitch is acute, grave, or intermediate.[2] A detailed investigation of these matters belongs to the study of meters.

A syllable is a sound without meaning which is composed of mutes and letters with a sound of their own, for GR can be a syllable without the A, or with it as in GRA. The investigation of syllables also belongs to metrical studies.

A connective [3] is a sound without meaning which neither prevents the formation of a significant combination of sounds (into a phrase) nor itself makes such a combination, and which, in a single phrase, cannot stand at the beginning, as for example μέν, δή, τοί, δέ. It may also be a sound without meaning which has the natural capacity of making a meaningful combination of several meaningful sounds, as, for example, ἀμφί, περί, etc.

An article is a sound without meaning of its own which indicates the beginning or the end or the divisions of a sentence.

1457 a

---

[1] Aristotle means that a semivowel has a distinct sound of its own, though it cannot be pronounced without a vowel to follow; a mute, on the other hand, merges with the vowel and its sound cannot be clearly distinguished.

[2] The aspirate was indicated by the rough breathing symbol over the initial vowel (the soft breathing only signifies the absence of an aspirate); the pitch was indicated by the Greek accents: the acute accent indicates that the voice rises, the grave that it falls, and the circumflex indicates a rise followed by a fall. It is a combination of both rather than, as Aristotle calls it, a mean between the two.

[3] Connectives include both conjunctives and connective particles on the one hand, and prepositions on the other. The text of this section is uncertain and I here mainly follow Bywater. The preposition only acquires meaning in combination with other words: e.g., go *to* the city, be *in* bed, etc.

Its natural place is at the beginning, the middle, or the end of a phrase.[4]

A noun [5] is a meaningful combination of sounds of which no part has a meaning of its own; it gives no indication of time. Even in a compound noun the parts are not used as having a meaning of their own: in the noun Theodorus, the second part loses its own meaning.

A verb is a meaningful combination of sounds which gives an indication of time; no part of it has a meaning of its own, just as in nouns. "Man" or "white" has no connotation of time, but "walks" or "walked" [6] indicates present or past time.

An inflected form of a noun or verb indicates, in the genitive, the idea of possession, in the dative the idea of advantage, and so on, or the singular or plural as in "man" and "men"; or it may indicate a mode of utterance, a question or an order: "walked" [7] or "walk" (in the imperative) are this kind of inflected forms of a verb.

A statement [8] is a meaningful combination of sounds, some of which have a meaning of their own. Only some, for not every statement consists of verbs and nouns: the definition of man, for example. It is possible to have a statement without a verb, but some parts of the statement will always have a meaning of their own. In the statement "Cleon walks," the

4 Again the text is very uncertain and some editors omit the article altogether. If in the text, it must here include the demonstrative pronoun, which indeed the Greek article seems originally to have been. We have no word that would indicate both.

5 Ὄνομα is certainly intended to include adjectives. For Theodorus we might substitute "Davidson."

6 Aristotle uses the perfect, which in Greek is an inflected form; but the literal translation "has walked" is not one word, and so would miss the point.

7 This makes no better sense in Greek than in English, for Greek had no inflected form to indicate a question. Aristotle is being careless.

8 The Greek word is λόγος, which can be a statement or a whole speech. This makes the illustration of the *Iliad* more natural in Greek.

word "Cleon" has a meaning of its own. The unity of a statement can be understood in two ways: the whole *Iliad* can be
said to be one because its parts are connected, but the definition of man is one because it indicates one thing.

XXI

Compound Words and Metaphors

A noun is either simple or compound. A simple noun is
made up of sounds that have no meaning in themselves, e.g.,
earth; a compound is made up of either a sound in itself
meaningless and one that has meaning (except that neither
retains its nature in the compound) or of sounds that in themselves have meaning. Such a compound could have three, four,
or more parts, as grandiose names do, e.g., Hermocaïcoxanthus.[1]

1457 b   A noun may be current, strange, metaphorical, ornamental,
newly coined, lengthened, abbreviated, or otherwise altered.
A current noun is one that everybody uses; a strange noun is
one used by another people so that, obviously, the same noun
can be both current and strange, but not to the same people.
The word *sigynon*, for example, is current among the
Cyprians for a spear, but it is strange to us.

A metaphor[2] is a word with some other meaning which is

---

[1] I have adopted Bywater's reading μεγαλειωτῶν, but the text is uncertain. The proper name Hermocaïcoxanthus seems to be a compound
made up of three river names: Hermus, Caïcus, and Xanthus.

[2] Aristotle uses the word metaphor in a wider sense than we do,
for almost any kind of transference (which is the etymological meaning of the word), and this is especially obvious where he classifies the
different kinds, for his classification is very formal and seems to miss
the main point, which is that a comparison is involved. The transference from species to genus may be merely the use of a term in an
unusual sense (συνεκδοχή) as of the part for the whole (μετωνυμία) and so
on. Even Aristotle's prized "proportional metaphor," a : b :: c : d, so that
you can apply d to a and b to c, is sometimes unsatisfactory—the cup as
the shield of Dionysus, for example. Yet the discussions of metaphor

transferred either from genus to species, or from species to genus, or from one species to another, or used by analogy. An example of transference from genus to species is: "There stands my ship," for to lie at anchor is a species of standing. From species to genus: "Odysseus did a thousand noble deeds," for "a thousand" stands here for many. From one species to another: "with the bronze drawing out his life" and "cutting with the stubborn bronze," for here drawing out and cutting both mean removing something. A proportional metaphor means that of four things the second is to the first as the fourth is to the third. The fourth can then be used for the second, or the second for the fourth, and sometimes the term to which the transferred term was related may be added. For example: the cup is to Dionysus what the shield is to Ares; one may then speak of the cup as the shield of Dionysus, or of the shield as the cup of Ares. Or again: old age is to life as evening is to the day; one may then speak of the evening as the day's old age, or of old age as the evening of life or the sunset of life, as Empedocles said. At times there may be no name in use for some of the terms of the analogy, but we can use this kind of metaphor none the less. For example, to cast seed is to sow, but there is no special word for the casting of rays by the sun; yet this is to the sunlight as sowing is to seed, and therefore it has been said of the sun that it is "sowing its divine rays." This kind of metaphor can also be used in a different way; one may add the quality which belongs to the transferred term in its proper setting, and then negative this quality, as if one called the shield not the cup of Ares but the wineless cup.

A new coinage is a word used by the poet but by no one else. There are a few such words, as when ἐρνύγες is used for κέρατα (horns), or ἀρητήρ for ἱερεύς (priest). A lengthened word is one in which a normally short vowel has been lengthened   1458 a

---

here and in *Rhetoric* 3, chs. 2 and 10 are of great interest and most of what Aristotle says throws a great deal of light on the use of metaphor in our more restricted sense.

or a syllable inserted, e.g., πόληος for πόλεως or Πηληιάδεω for Πηλείδου; a shortened word is one from which some part is omitted, e.g., κρῖ, δῶ, or in μία γίνεται ἀμφοτέρων ὄψ. An altered word is one in which part is left unaltered, but part of it is changed, e.g., δεξιτερὸν κατὰ μάζον instead of δεξιόν.[3]

Of the nouns themselves, some are masculine, some feminine, and some neuter. Masculine are those ending in ν, ρ, ς, and the two letter compounds of ς, namely ψ and ξ. Nouns which end in vowels which are always long, such as η and ω, or a lengthened α are feminine, so that the masculine and feminine endings are equal in number, since ψ and ξ are the same as ς. No noun ends with a mute, nor with a vowel that is always short (ε and ο). Only three nouns end in ι, namely μέλι (honey), κόμμι (gum), and πέπερι (pepper); while five end in υ. These endings belong to neuter nouns, which also end in ν and ς.

XXII

Excellence of Diction

Diction, to be good, should be clear without being common. Now the clearest language consists of current words, but it is common. The poetry of Cleophon and Sthenelus is an ex-

---

[3] The last phrase is from Homer *Iliad* 5.393, where Hera is said to have been wounded "in the right breast"; κρῖ for κριθή (barley) and δῶ for δῶμα (house) are also epic abbreviations and are found, for example, in *Iliad* 8.564 and 1.426 respectively. ὄψ for ὄψις (eye or face) is quoted from Empedocles (fr. 88, Diels). πόληος and Πηλιάδεω are epic genitives; ἀρητήρ is used in *Iliad* 1.11, but ἐρνύγες is unknown.

The short paragraph which follows (some editors condemn it as spurious) on the gender of nouns according to their endings is somewhat unsatisfactory. Aristotle himself first gives ν and ς as masculine endings, and then as neuter. Bywater suggests (note *ad loc.*) that these classifications arose from that of proper names into masculine and feminine, for there the masculine and feminine endings are as stated. When applied to nouns as a whole, however, there are a great many exceptions. The form of the nouns that Aristotle has in mind is of course the nominative singular. The passage may serve to remind us that the art of grammar was still included both in poetics and rhetoric.

ample of this. Unusual words, on the other hand, give dignity to the language and avoid colloquialism. By unusual I mean strange words, metaphors, lengthened forms, anything contrary to current usage; but if all one's language is of this nature, the result is riddles or gibberish; riddles if it consists wholly of metaphors, gibberish if it consists entirely of rare words. The essence of a riddle is to express facts by combining them in an impossible way; this cannot be done by the mere arrangement of words but requires the use of metaphor, as in "I saw a man by means of fire welding bronze upon another," [1] and the like. A mass of rare words is gibberish.

What we need is a mixed diction. On the one hand, the use of unusual, metaphorical, ornamental words, and of the other kinds mentioned above, avoids commonness and colloquialism; current vocabulary, on the other hand, makes for clarity. Lucid yet noncolloquial language results in large part from using nouns in lengthened, shortened, or altered forms, for these, while avoiding the colloquial by being unusual, yet remain near enough the usual to retain clarity. It is a mistake to criticize this manner of expression and to make fun of the poet, as old Eucleides did: he said that it was easy to write poetry if one was allowed to lengthen syllables at will, a process he lampooned in these very words: Ἐπιχάρην εἶδον Μαραθῶνάδε βαδίζοντα and also by: οὐκ ἄν γ' ἐράμενος τὸν ἐκείνου ἐλλέβορον.[2] Too obvious a use of this license is indeed

1458 b

1 Aristotle explains that this refers to the process of cupping in *Rhetoric* 3, ch. 2.
2 As Eucleides was deliberately writing metrical nonsense, these lines do not scan. However, we can turn the first ("I saw Epichares walking to Marathon") into a hexameter by improperly lengthening the first syllable of Ἐπιχάρην and βαδίζοντα i.e., $- \cup \cup | - - | - \cup \cup | - \cup \cup | - - | - -$. The second is more confusing, but as only the lengthening of syllables is mentioned, we can scan it as a hexameter of a kind by lengthening the first syllable of ἐράμενος and the middle syllables of ἐλλέβορον, i.e., $- - | - \cup \cup | - \cup \cup | - - | - - | - -$. The very poor ending with three spondees is probably deliberate. The meaning of this line is obscure, it has something to do with a lover and hellebore, but no verb is expressed in the line, and the meaning is clearly incomplete.

ridiculous, but moderation applies to writing in all its parts. Eucleides could have achieved the same effect from the inopportune and deliberately ridiculous use of metaphors, strange words, and all other devices. But what a difference the appropriate use of lengthened forms can make will be seen if we insert the common words into epic verses. So too with rare words, metaphors, and other devices, as anyone can see if he puts the common words in their place. For example, we have the same iambic line in Aeschylus and Euripides, with the change of one word, a rare word replacing a common one, and the result is that one line is beautiful, the other cheap. The line of Aeschylus is in the *Philoctetes*:

"This cancerous sore is eating up my flesh";

but Euripides wrote "feasting on" instead of "eating up." Then again, take the line:

"Of no account, unseemly, and unnoted,"

and replace this by current words:

"Feeble and ugly, and quite unconsidered."

Or take:

"He set a table sparse and couch unseemly,"

and replace it by:

"He set a little table and an ugly stool";

or if one changed: "the shores resound" into "the shores make a noise." Ariphrades ridiculed the tragic poets in his comedies because they use language which no one would use in conversation, they use such expressions as δωμάτων ἄπο (instead of ἀπὸ δωμάτων), σέθεν, ἐγὼ δέ νιν, Ἀχιλλέως πέρι (instead of περὶ Ἀχιλλέως), and others of the same kind.[3] All these forms, precisely because they are not in common use, lift the language of poetry out of the ordinary. This Ariphrades did not realize.

It is important, however, that each of these devices should

1459 a

---

[3] The point of the first example ("from the house") is that the preposition follows the noun instead of preceding it, and so with the last ("about Achilles"). σέθεν is an epic form of the genitive singular of the second person personal pronoun, and νιν is similarly an old form of the third person singular pronoun.

be used with a sense of propriety. This is true of both compound and rare words, but metaphorical language is the most
important. The right use of metaphors is a sign of inborn
talent and cannot be learned from anyone else; it comes from
the ability to observe similarities in things.

Compound nouns are most appropriate in dithyramb,
strange words in epic, and metaphors in iambic verse. Moreover, all the above devices are useful in the epic, whereas in
iambic verse, as it is the closest imitation of ordinary speech,
those nouns are appropriate which one might use in conversation, that is, current, metaphorical, and ornamental words.

We have now said enough about tragedy and the art of
imitation through acting.

XXIII

The Epic

Imitation through narrative in verse obviously must, like
tragedy, have a dramatic plot structure; it must be concerned
with one complete action, it must have a beginning, middles,
and an end, in order that the whole narrative may attain the
unity of a living organism and provide its own peculiar kind
of pleasure. Its structure must be different from that of his-
tories. History has to expound not one action but one period
of time and all that happens within this period to one or more
persons, however tenuous the connection between one event
and the others. The battle of Salamis and that of the
Carthaginians in Sicily took place at the same time, but they
had no common purpose; similarly, events may follow one
another in time without having any common end in view. Yet
nearly all our epic poets adopt this historical structure.[1]

In this, as previously mentioned, Homer is an immortal
compared with other poets. He did not take the whole Trojan
war as his subject, though it had a beginning, a middle, and
an end, because it would have been too large a subject which
could not be grasped as a whole, or, if he had kept his poem

[1] For this unsatisfactory attitude to history cp. ch. 9, and note 1 above.

to a moderate length, the variety of events would have made it too involved. As it is, he selected one part of the war as his subject, and he incorporated many of the other events of the war into his work as incidents—the catalogue of ships, for example, and others. The other poets focus their work upon one person, or one period of time, or one action with many 1459 b parts, like the authors of the *Cypria* and the *Little Iliad*. That is why the *Iliad* and the *Odyssey* each furnish the subject of only one tragedy, or at most two, while the *Cypria* has provided the subjects of many tragedies, and the *Little Iliad* has given us more than eight: *The Award of Achilles' Armor, Philoctetes, Neoptolemus, Eurypylus, Odysseus as a Beggar, The Spartan Women, The Sack of Troy, The Sailing of the Fleet, Sinon,* and *The Trojan Women*.[2]

XXIV

The Epic—continued

Further, the different types of epic should be the same as the types of tragedy; either simple or complex, either an epic of character or of suffering.[1] The elements, too, except for music and spectacle, are the same. Epic requires reversals, recognitions, and scenes of suffering. The thought and diction

2 The *Cypria* and the *Little Iliad* were poems of the epic cycle, i.e., the non-Homeric early epics of which only very few and scrappy fragments remain. Of the plays mentioned we have only the *Philoctetes* of Sophocles and the *Trojan Women* of Euripides.

1 Critics have been puzzled by this classification which seems to imply a previous classification of tragedy into these four kinds, and some have wanted to identify them with the four types or kinds of ch. 18, but we saw that the simple tragedy does not fit these (note 2). I doubt if Aristotle intends an exhaustive classification here. This is a rapid survey of similarities between epic and tragedy. He makes the general statement that epic and tragedy have the same forms, and *illustrates* it by mentioning four kinds or forms, all of which have at one time or another been applied to tragedy. These are especially significant here because they are the basis of the comparison between the *Iliad* and the *Odyssey* which follows. They are here apparently opposites; simple is obviously the opposite of complex, and "ethical" seems to be opposed to "pathetic." See next note.

must be good. All these are found first in Homer, and he uses them well. As for the plot structure of each poem, the *Iliad* is simple and an epic of suffering, the *Odyssey* is complex (it has recognition throughout) and an epic of character.[2] Moreover, they surpass all other epics in diction and thought.

Epic differs from tragedy in the length of its plot and in its meter. We have already indicated the adequate limit of length, namely, that one must be able to grasp the whole, from beginning to end, as a unity. This could be so if the plots were shorter than those of the ancient epics, and corresponded to the length of the tragedies a poet presents for one performance.[3] The epic has a special and important feature which allows its length to be greater: tragedy cannot represent different parts of the action at the same time but only that part which is enacted upon the stage, whereas the epic, being narrative in form, can make different parts of the action come

[2] This comparison is curiously expressed. That the *Iliad* has a simple plot, i.e., one without reversal or recognition, we may agree (though one might see reversal where Achilles sends Patroclus into battle), and also that it has more *pathos* both in the sense of suffering and of passion. It is also true that the *Odyssey* has a more complex plot in the Aristotelian sense of a plot with recognition scenes. That the Odyssey is more "ethical," however, is more startling, for if by this is meant that it has better characterization, this is simply not true. The word ἦθος, however, which has hitherto meant character and characterization, and which originally referred to speaking or writing in character, came to mean, in rhetorical criticism, to speak more naturally, as the writing in character (such as in Lysias, for example) came to be opposed to the forceful and passionate kind of writing of Demosthenes. Hence it also meant to speak more naturally, in a lower key, without grandeur or passion. This meaning is well established in later texts (e.g., Quintilian 6.2.8-24), and clearly something of this meaning attaches to the word here, for Aristotle must mean that the *Odyssey* is less passionate and elevated. A parallel contrast between the two epics is found in Longinus' famous essay (see my *Longinus On Great Writing*, "Library of Liberal Arts," No. 79), p. 16 and note 10.

For Aristotle's treatment of the epic see Introduction, pp. xii-xiii.

[3] That is, three tragedies and also, presumably, the satyric drama which followed, each of these being about 1200-1500 lines. The four together would be less than half the length of the *Iliad* or the *Odyssey*. It is interesting to note that the *Argonautica* of Apollonius of Rhodes conforms to Aristotle's suggested length.

to a head simultaneously, so that these scenes, appropriate to
the epic, increase the bulk of the poem. Thus the epic has an
advantage which contributes to its grandeur, enables it to vary
the story for the audience, and to illustrate it by diverse incidents. For monotony soon satiates and causes tragedies to
fail in the theater.

The suitability of the heroic hexameter was discovered by
experience. Should anyone attempt to write narrative poetry
in any other meter or combination of meters, the result would
appear incongruous. The heroic meter is the most steady and
weighty of all; this is why, above all others, it admits rare
words and metaphors, for narrative poetry is different from all
others. Iambic verse and the trochaic tetrameter express
motion and excitement; the former is the meter of action, the
latter of the dance. To mix all these meters, as Chaeremon
did, would be even more absurd. No one has, therefore,
written a long poetic narrative in any other than the heroic
meter. As we said before, nature herself teaches us to choose
the appropriate meter.[4]

1460 a

Apart from his many other qualities, Homer deserves praise
because he alone realizes when he should write in his own
person. A poet should himself say very little, for he is not then
engaged in imitation.[5] Now the others take a personal part

4 Chaeremon is also mentioned in the first chapter as having written a
metrical medley. The reference in the last sentence is to ch. 4.

5 At the beginning of ch. 3, when discussing the differences in the
means of imitation, Aristotle distinguished dramatic performances (impersonation) from narrative. The latter he subdivided into (a) the narrator
speaks in his own person, and (b) he takes on another personality, as
Homer does (ch. 4, note 2). Actually, Homer only speaks in his own
person in the few invocations to the Muse and the very rare addresses to
a hero in the vocative. The introduction before Chryses speaks is, after
the invocation, straight narrative. Aristotle, in both passages, expresses
himself carelessly. In neither passage does he clearly distinguish between
the poet speaking in his own person and straight narrative, for obviously
he does *not* mean that other poets spoke in their own person nearly all
the time instead of writing straight narrative. He clearly means they did
not use direct speech as Homer did. It is only when speaking strictly in
his own person that the poet can be said not to imitate, for narration *is*

throughout, and let their characters speak only occasionally and say very little; but Homer, after a brief introduction, straightway brings on a man or woman or some other speaking character—not one of them without characteristic traits.

The Marvelous and the Inexplicable

Tragedy should make men marvel, but the epic, in which the audience does not witness the action, has greater scope for the inexplicable, at which men marvel most. The circumstances of the pursuit of Hector in the *Iliad*, for example, would appear ridiculous on the stage, with some actors standing still while Achilles signals to them to keep away, but in the epic this incongruity goes unnoticed. To marvel is pleasant, as can be seen from the fact that everybody adds something in telling a story, thinking to please.

Above all, Homer has taught other poets to tell an untrue story as it should be told, by taking advantage of a logical fallacy. When one event is followed by a second as a consequence or concomitant, men are apt to infer, when the second event happens, that the first must have happened or be happening, though the inference is false. If, then, the first event is not true but, if it were true, the second would necessarily have happened or be happening, we should establish the second if we want the first to be believed. For our mind, knowing the second to be true, falsely infers the truth of the first. An example of this can be found in the bath scene of the *Odyssey*.[6]

What is impossible but can be believed should be preferred to what is possible but unconvincing. The plot should not

imitation, unless indeed the word "imitator" ($\mu\iota\mu\eta\tau\dot{\eta}s$) means here, as in ch. 3, "impersonator."

[6] The bath scene (as before) is the nineteenth book of the *Odyssey*. Because Odysseus can describe certain apparel that he himself once wore Penelope assumes his whole tale that he is a Cretan who met Odysseus to be true (165-248). The logical fallacy is that Penelope reasons as follows: "If the stranger's tale were true he would be able to describe what Odysseus wore; he can describe what Odysseus wore; therefore his tale is true."

consist of inexplicable incidents; as far as possible it should contain nothing inexplicable. If this is not possible, the inexplicable should lie outside the part of the story that is dramatized, like Oedipus' ignorance of the manner in which Laius died, and not be in the play itself, like the account of the Pythian games in Sophocles' *Electra,* or in the *Mysians* the man who came from Tegea to Mysia without saying a word.[7] It is ridiculous to say that the plot would have been ruined without these incidents. Such a plot should not be chosen in the first place, but if it was chosen and a more reasonable outcome seems possible, the plot is also absurd. The inexplicable manner in which Odysseus was put ashore [8] would have appeared obviously intolerable if written by a lesser poet. As it is, the poet's other excellences make the incident acceptable and hide its absurdity.

1460 b

Elaborate diction should be reserved for those parts which have little action, little presentation of character and thought, for over-brilliant language obscures both character and thought.

XXV

Problems of Criticism

We turn now to the problems raised by critics and the way to solve them. The following examination will clarify their nature and the classes into which they fall. Since the poet, like

[7] Oedipus' ignorance of the circumstances of the murder of Laius dates from his arrival in Thebes years before, and is therefore part of the situation when the play begins. In the reference to Sophocles' *Electra* it is not clear whether Aristotle means that if the news of the death of Orestes were true, Clytemnestra would have heard the news before and that therefore her credulity is inexplicable, or whether he is objecting to the anachronism, since there were no Pythian games in her day. The former seems more probable and makes a better contrast to Oedipus' ignorance. *The Mysians* is a lost play by Aeschylus.

[8] *Odyssey* 13. 70-124. King Antinous sends Odysseus home in one of the magic Phaeacian ships, and the journey is accomplished in an incredibly short time. This is made easier by the fact that Odysseus is asleep throughout the voyage, and still asleep when put ashore by the Phaeacians, who then return home.

the painter and other makers of images, is an imitator, the object of his imitation must always be represented in one of three ways: as it was or is, as it is said or thought to be, or as it ought to be.

He communicates this by means of language, with the addition, it may be, of rare words and metaphors. We allow the poet many modifications of language. What is right for a politician is not right for a poet; indeed, what is right for a poet is not the same as for any other craftsman.

Intrinsic and Incidental Flaws

In poetry itself there are two kinds of flaw, one of which is intrinsic, the other incidental. If a poet chooses a subject for imitation and cannot represent it, that is an intrinsic flaw in his art. But if the mistake lies in the subject as he meant to imitate it and he represents, for example, a horse putting both right feet forward at once, or he makes some other mistake which belongs to the technique of another art—an error in medicine or the like—and this leads to some impossibility in his work, that is an incidental flaw.[1] It is in the light of this distinction that we should seek the solution of critical problems.

First, flaws that are intrinsic in the poetic art. If the poet represents something impossible, it is an error, but he is right if the poetry achieves its own purpose, which has already been explained, if, done in this way, the effect either of the passage concerned or of another part of the poem is more startling. An example of this is the pursuit of Hector. On the other hand, if the poetic purpose can be achieved as well or better without doing violence to the technical correctness concerned, then the passage is wrong, for one should avoid every kind of

[1] By "the mistake lies in the subject" Aristotle seems to mean the subject as the poet sees it in his mind's eye. If he *thinks* that a horse walks by moving both right feet, and otherwise makes a good picture of such a horse, it is an incidental flaw. But if, knowing his subject, he makes a bad picture of it, his art is at fault. The words for flaw are here also ἁμαρτία, and its cognate ἁμάρτημα.

error where possible. We should ask what kind of flaw it is, whether one of poetic art or an incidental flaw in respect to something else. It is a lesser fault not to know that a hind has no horns than to make a bad picture of it.

Poetry and Truth

Then there is also the criticism that what the poet says is not true. This can perhaps be answered in the words of Sophocles when he said that he made his characters what they ought to be, while Euripides made them what they were. If the representation is not of either of these kinds, the answer may be that this is what men say it is as, for example, in the stories told about the gods: these may be neither better than the truth nor true, and Xenophanes may be right; [2] but that is what men believe. Or perhaps it is not better so, but it used to be so, as in the passage about the arms, where Homer says: "The spears were standing upright on their spikes," for it was then the custom to place the spears so, as today among the Illyrians.

1461 a

The Representation of Evil

As to whether anything which is said or done is right or not, one should not consider only whether that particular statement or action is good or bad, but the character of the person speaking or acting, the other person affected or addressed, the time, the means, and the purpose, as, for example, to realize a greater good or avoid a greater evil.

Criticisms of Diction

Other criticisms may be met by examining the words used. In the expression οὐρῆας μὲν πρῶτον ("first the mules"), the word οὐρῆες does not, perhaps, refer to mules but to sentinels.[3] So

---

[2] Xenophanes is the poet-philosopher who attacked Homer for his wicked tales about the gods about 500 B.C. For this broadening of the concept of imitation see Introduction, pp. xviii-xix, and for the next paragraph, on evil in drama, see Introduction, p. xx.

[3] The Greek examples in this section can be explained, but they cannot

where Dolon is said to be εἶδος . . κακός (bad looking), this may
mean not that his body is ill-proportioned but that his face is
ugly, for the Cretans use the word εὐειδής (beautiful) to de-
note beautiful features only.[4] And again, the phrase ζωρότερον
δὲ κέραιε may not mean "mix a stronger wine," as drunkards
take wine unmixed, but "mix the wine more quickly." [5]

Or certain expressions may be metaphorical, as for example
"All other gods and men were sleeping through the night,"
and the poet goes on to say: "He would look toward the
Trojan plain (wonder at the many fires and hear) the confused
noise of pipes and flutes." Here the word "all" is used metaphorically, for all is a species of many.[6] The phrase "alone

---

be translated. It may therefore be helpful to summarize the section here
for the general reader. Aristotle points out that certain criticisms of
diction may be met by pointing out that (1) a word is used in an unusual
sense, or (2) metaphorically; that (3) a change of pitch or accent, or (4)
the right punctuation may give the right meaning; or it may be a question of (5) resolving an ambiguity, (6) of usage, or (7) of the precise
meaning of a word.

The first example refers to *Iliad* 1. 50, where the angry Apollo sends a
plague upon the Greek host, and first directs his disease-laden arrows
"upon the mules." A critic had obviously asked, why the innocent mules?
Aristotle's explanation is, however, unlikely, for the god is said to have
sent his arrows "then upon [the men] themselves," and "sentinels" would
not provide the obviously intended contrast. It is more likely that the
poet had in mind the fact that pack animals may be carriers of disease.

[4] Objection had presumably been taken to *Iliad* 10.316 on the ground
that if Dolon had a bad physique he could not have been a swift
runner, which he is also said to be. The objection seems groundless,
though Aristotle's reply that the word may here refer only to the face
throws an interesting light upon the Greek conception of physical beauty,
our own usage of the word beautiful being more like the Cretan, but
Aristotle's suggestion seems contrary to Homeric usage.

[5] The reference is to words addressed by Achilles to Patroclus when he
is receiving the Greek envoys in *Iliad* 9.202. The objection seems to have
been to strong drink under the circumstances, as the Greeks drank their
wine mixed with water. Again, however, the suggestion of Aristotle seems
improbable.

[6] Aristotle is obviously speaking from memory and he is confusing two
passages, one at the beginning of Iliad 2, where we are told that the

shares not" is also metaphorical, for the best known is said to be the only one.[7] Or there may be a difference of pronunciation, as Hippias solved the difficulty in δίδομεν δέ οἱ and τὸ μὲν οὐ καταπύθεται ὄμβρῳ.[8] Punctuation may give the answer in some cases, as when Empedocles wrote: "Quickly things grew mortal which before knew immortality, and things pure before were mixed."[9] In other cases we should realize the am-

---

other men and gods were asleep but Zeus was thinking of his promise to Thetis, and the beginning of the tenth book, where we are told that the other Achaeans were asleep, but Agamemnon was awake, looking over the plain to the campfires and hearing sounds. The word "all" does not occur in our texts in either passage. Aristotle here tries to explain the discrepancy he thought he remembered (or he may have read πάντες in 2.1) by trying to reduce it to a metaphor from genus to species.

[7] The reference is to *Iliad* 18.489, where the constellation of the Great Bear is said "alone not to share in the baths of the Ocean," i.e., not to set. But there are other stars that do not set. Aristotle again wants to reduce this to a metaphor from genus to species, "best known" being a kind of "alone" (see above ch. 21).

[8] The first of these two references is to *Iliad* 2.15, though it does not exactly correspond to our texts. It is the passage in which Zeus sends a lying dream to Agamemnon to tell him that the gods will grant him the capture of Troy now, if he fights at once. This is not true. Contemporary critics presumably had objected to this conduct on Zeus' part, as many have since. By shifting the accent and reading διδόμεν (infinitive used as imperative) Zeus does not say "we grant him," but tells the dream to do so. This attempt to shift the responsibility to Dream does not really seem to exonerate Zeus, as Dream would still be acting under his instructions.

The second phrase is from *Iliad* 23.328, where Nestor gives advice to his son on how to win the chariot race. The reference is to a tree stump marking the turning point. If we read οὗ the meaning is that part *of it* is rotted by rain; if we read οὐ (the negative), it means that the stump is *not* rotting. Commentators are not agreed as to which was the reading suggested by Hippias.

[9] The quotation is from a fragment of Empedocles (88, Diels), and the point is whether "before" (πρίν) goes with the words that follow or precede it, i.e., either "things were pure which were mixed before," or "things were mixed which were pure before"; there can be little doubt that Empedocles meant the latter, but the point is that there is a possible ambiguity.

biguity, as in "more than two thirds of the night had gone, and a third of it was left." [10]

Some difficulties may be solved by an appeal to customary usage. Just as wine mixed with water is called wine, so Homer speaks of "a greave of new-wrought tin," [11] workers in iron are called χαλκεῖς (workers in bronze), and Ganymede is said to be wine server to Zeus, though it is not wine that the gods drink. This, however, might be a metaphor.[12]

Where a contradiction seems to be involved, we should observe the different senses which a word may bear, as in "and the bronze spear was stopped there" we should consider in how many senses a spear may be stopped.[13]

The Right Critical Attitude

We should interpret these passages in a manner contrary to that mentioned by Glaucon, who says that critics make certain unreasonable assumptions, condemn the poet out of hand, and then argue on that basis; they blame him for saying what they think he said if it contradicts their own ideas. That is

1461 b

---

[10] Iliad 10.252-3: παροίχωκεν δὲ πλέω νὺξ / τῶν δύο μοιράων, τριτάτη δ' ἔτι μοῖρα λέλειπται. The problem seems to be that if more than two thirds of the night have gone, one third cannot remain! The solution is somewhat obscure but it appears to be to take πλέω in some other sense, "the full two thirds," or the like.

[11] Iliad 21.592: κνημὶς νεοτεύκτου κασσιτέροιο. The greave is called "of well-wrought tin" though they were in fact made of a mixture of tin and copper; this Aristotle compares to the use of wine to indicate a mixture of wine and water.

[12] That is, οἰνοχοεύειν is used in the general sense of "to serve a drink," instead of "serving wine." Or, if we explain it as a metaphor, then as wine is to men, so is nectar to the gods, and we may therefore call nectar the wine of the gods.

[13] In Iliad 20.272, the shield of Achilles is said to have three layers of bronze, two of tin and one of gold. This last must obviously be on the outside, yet we are told that the spear of Aeneas pierced two layers but also was "stopped" in the gold. Aristotle presumably means that the spear may be said to be "stopped" by the outside layer even if the point penetrates two further layers.

what happened about Icarius, the father of Penelope. They think he was a Spartan, and then argue from this that it is absurd that Telemachus should not have met him on his journey to Sparta. However, the Cephalonians may be right; they say that Odysseus married one of their compatriots, and that his wife's father's name was Icadius and not Icarius at all. The difficulty here is probably due to a mistake.

Generally speaking, we must judge the impossible in relation to its poetic effect, to what is morally better, or to accepted opinion. As regards poetic effect, the impossible that can be believed should be preferred to what is possible but unconvincing. There are, we are told, no such men as Zeuxis painted; true, but he paints them better than life, and the ideal model should be better than the actual reality. The inexplicable in poetry may also be justified by reference to what men say exists; and sometimes, when rightly interpreted, it is found not to be inexplicable at all, for it is also likely that unlikely things should happen.

Contradictions should be examined as is done when refuting an argument, whether the two statements refer to the same thing, in the same relation and in the same sense, so that we can be sure it is the poet who contradicts what he has said in his own person, or that it is contrary to what an intelligent person would assume from what has been said.

It is right, however, to criticize a poet for what is inexplicable or evil whenever these appear without need or benefit; the introduction of Aegeus in the *Medea* of Euripides is inexplicable and the wickedness of his Menelaus in the *Orestes* is unnecessary.

Unfavorable criticisms, then, come under five heads: that what the poet has written is impossible, inexplicable, harmful, contradictory, or artistically wrong. The solutions of these difficulties must be looked for in the ways we have suggested, and these are twelve in number.[14]

14 What these twelve ways of answering criticism are has taxed the ingenuity of commentators, as can be seen in Bywater's notes.

XXVI

Tragedy and Epic

One might be at a loss to know whether epic or tragic imitation is the more worthy. For, the argument runs, if the less vulgar art is the better, and that art is less vulgar which appeals to a better kind of audience, it very obviously follows that the art which does everything by impersonation is vulgar. For it is the realization that their audience does not understand unless they make additions of their own which leads the tragic actors to indulge in every kind of gesticulation, like second-rate flute players who whirl themselves around when they imitate discus throwing, or drag their chorus leader about when they are playing Scylla. And so tragedy is a vulgar art. So, too, the older actors looked upon their successors, as when Mynniscus called Callipides an ape because of his exaggerated acting; and the same opinion is held about Pindarus. As these two kinds of actors are to one another, so tragedy is to the epic. The epic, they tell us, is directed to a more select audience who do not need these antics, whereas tragedy is directed to an inferior audience. And if it is vulgar, it is obviously less worthy. 1462 a

Now in the first place this criticism does not apply to the tragedy, but to the acting, for a rhapsode too can overdo the gestures when reciting epic, as Sosistratus did, and so can a singer in a contest, as did Mnasitheus of Opuntium. Moreover, not every kind of gesture is to be deprecated—one would not condemn the dance—but only those of worthless men, as Callipides was blamed, and other actors are today, for acting the part of women in a base manner. Then again, tragedy can achieve its effect without any kind of gesture, just as the epic can. You can tell what kind of a tragedy it is by reading it. It follows that if tragedy is superior in other respects, it is not necessarily subject to this weakness.

In the second place, tragedy contains all the elements of the epic—it can even use epic meter—and besides these, it has

the important elements of music which stirs us to pleasure most vividly, and of spectacle. Indeed, it has vividness both in the reading and the performance. And it fulfills the purpose of
1462 b   its imitation in a smaller compass. The more compact is more pleasing than that which is spread over a great length of time. Imagine someone giving the *Oedipus* of Sophocles as many verses as the *Iliad!*

Epic imitation has less unity; indeed, any epic provides the subject matter for several tragedies. If an epic poet chooses one story, either he must present it briefly and his poem comes to an abrupt end, or he follows the length proper to his meter and his subject is watered down. The epic contains several actions—and both the *Iliad* and the *Odyssey* have many such parts with a length of their own, even though those two poems are constructed in the best possible way and are the imitation of one action as far as an epic can be.

If, then, tragedy excels in all these ways and also in its artistic function, for no art must arouse just any kind of pleasure but only that which is appropriate to it, then tragedy achieves its purpose better and is superior to the epic.

So much for tragedy and the epic, their kinds and their elements, the number and differences of these, the causes of success and failure, the problems raised by critics, and their solution.

ON STYLE

[RHETORIC, BOOK III, Chapters 1-12]

ON STYLE

[Rhetoric, Book Three, Chapters I-XII]

Plato had said that if rhetoric was to be a *technê* (an art or craft based on special knowledge) the speaker or writer should have knowledge of the human soul and its different parts or functions; he should also have a theoretical knowledge of the different types of arguments, and of their appeal to different kinds of men (*Phaedrus* 269d and 271d-272b).

Aristotle took up this challenge in the first two books of the *Rhetoric*. He begins by asserting that rhetoric *is* a *technê,* and establishes the formula of the three types of rhetoric which was universally adopted later; these types are (1) the deliberative or political, (2) the forensic, and (3) the epideictic oratory of display. He then proceeds to an analysis of human goods and the external circumstances of human life which the orator must know. In the second book he deals with human emotions such as anger, fear, pity (ch. 8), indignation, etc., the different characteristics of youth, middle, and old age, and the ways various men react to power, wealth, and so on. Having done this, he goes on to a study of commonplaces upon which arguments are based, and analyzes different kinds of proof, refutation and *enthymêma* (i.e., the reasoning from probable premises which is to rhetoric what the syllogism is to philosophy, *Rhet.* 1. 2. 8-9).

The third book consists of two parts. The first part deals with style (chs. 1-12), the second with *taxis,* i.e., the right order, purpose, and method of each of the necessary parts of a speech. It is the part on style which is here translated.

I

There are three subjects that need to be dealt with in connection with a speech: first, the sources of convincing arguments; second, matters of style; third, how to arrange the different parts of the speech. We have already dealt with the sources of convincing arguments; we have seen that they

1403 b

are of three kinds, what these kinds are, and why there are only three: men are persuaded either by their own feelings, or by the impression the speaker makes upon them, or again because something has been proved to them.[1] We have also dealt with rhetorical reasoning, and what it should be based on: the different kinds of reasoning, and the commonplaces. The next step is to discuss style, for it is not enough to know what should be said; it must be said in the right way, and many factors contribute to the impression made by a speech.

History of Style and Delivery

It was natural that men first investigated the problem which naturally presented itself first, namely, what means of persuasion could be found in the matter itself; and then stylistic arrangement. There is, however, a third factor of great consequence which has not yet been studied, namely, delivery. The study of this came late even in the production of tragedy and in public recitation, for at first the poets themselves acted in their tragedies. Obviously, delivery is also a factor in rhetoric, as well as in poetry where it has been studied by Glaucon of Teos among others.

Delivery is concerned with the use of the voice to express every emotion: when it should be loud, low, or in between, when its pitch should be shrill, deep, or intermediate, and what rhythms are appropriate in each case. There are three factors to investigate: the volume, the pitch, and the rhythm. Those who manage their voices well carry off the prizes. In the theater, the actors have today become more important than the poets; the same is true in public debate because our forms of government are depraved.[2]

---

[1] Cp. *Rhet.* 1.2.3.: "There are three kinds of convincing arguments provided through the speech: the first kind depends on the character of the speaker, the second on the feelings of his hearers, and the third depends on the speech itself, something is proved or appears to have been proved."

[2] I.e., the audiences are depraved, both in the theater and in the assemblies. Presumably Aristotle means here that inferior people have

Even the study of style developed late, and there is as yet no body of doctrine which could be called an "art" of delivery; the subject is considered vulgar, and rightly so. But the whole study of the art of rhetoric is concerned with people's opinions, and we must take delivery into account, not because it is right but because it is unavoidable. It is right, when speaking, to aim only at giving neither offense nor pleasure; it is right to debate only on the facts of the case and to look upon everything other than factual proof as irrelevant. Nevertheless these things are of consequence, as I said, because of the depravity of the audience. However, style and delivery[3] do hold a small and unavoidable place in every kind of instruction, and the subject is made more or less clear to some extent by the manner of exposition, but the difference is not so great. All these things are merely concerned with the appearance of truth and are directed to the hearer. This is why nobody teaches geometry that way. Whenever delivery comes to be developed as an art, it will have the same power as acting.

The subject has been cursorily treated by some, by Thrasymachus, for example, in his *Appeals to Pity*. To be an

1404 a

---

too much power in government. For similar sentiments see *Poetics* (end of ch. 13 and note 5), and Introduction, pp. x-xi.

[3] I have here translated λέξις by "style and delivery," because Aristotle has both ideas in mind, and both can be included under *lexis*. Whereas *logos* can refer to either form or content (or both), λέξις refers to form only, to the "manner of speaking" in the widest sense, or to any particular quality of manner or style, be it diction, word arrangement, presentation of material, delivery, or single phrases or indeed words, according to context. In the reference to the poets just below, and also at the beginning of ch. 2, it obviously refers to diction or language, as it mostly does up to and including ch. 8. On the other hand, in ch. 9 it clearly refers to word arrangement, while in chs. 10 and 11 it has the more general meaning of style. The translation must vary with the context if confusion is to be avoided. For examples of such confusion in Dionysius see my article "Thrasymachus, Theophrastus and Dionysius of Halicarnassus" in *American Journal of Philology*, 73 (1952), 254-267. The reader will there also find a discussion of Thrasymachus' contribution to style and criticism.

actor requires natural talent and is less a matter of training, but delivery in rhetoric is more a matter of training in the technique of the art. Gifted actors win the prizes, and so do orators trained in delivery. The power of the written word, too, depends on style rather than on content.

It was naturally the poets who first gave the impetus to these studies, for words represent things, and the voice is the most imitative of our faculties. Hence arose the arts of public recitation, acting, and the rest. And as the poets, though they said silly things,[4] were thought to have acquired their reputation through their diction, the language of prose was at first poetical, that of Gorgias for example. Even today uneducated people believe that those who express themselves poetically speak most beautifully, but this is not true, for the language of prose is different from that of poetry. And what has happened proves my point: not even tragic poets any longer use that kind of poetic diction. Just as they changed from the trochaic tetrameter to the iambic meter because this meter is the most similar to prose, so they have given up using other than current language, though earlier poets used to adorn their language with unusual words, as those who write in hexameters still do. It is absurd to imitate a diction which its originators have themselves given up. We need not, therefore, go into detail about every aspect of diction, but only mention those which apply to prose, which we are now discussing. Poetic diction has already been treated in the *Poetics*.[5]

II

The Right Diction

1404 b   Let us therefore consider these matters to have been dealt with, and let us define the excellence of style to be lucidity. This is proved by the fact that speech is not fulfilling its func-

4 For this supercilious attitude to poets see Introduction, pp. x-xi.

5 In ch. 22. The next chapter in part repeats what was said there. The two discussions of metaphor should be compared, and see also chs. 4 and 10 below. As in the *Poetics*, to write in hexameters means to write epic poetry.

tion unless its meaning is clear. The diction should be neither common nor too elevated for the subject, but appropriate. Poetic language may be said to avoid commonness, but it is unsuitable for prose. Current nouns and verbs [1] make for clarity, while the other kinds of words mentioned in the *Poetics* make the diction uncommon and ornamented, for the use of other than current language gives an appearance of dignity. Men feel toward language as they feel toward strangers and fellow citizens, and we must introduce an element of strangeness into our diction because people marvel at what is far away, and to marvel is pleasant. Many factors produce this effect in poetry and are there appropriate since the subjects and personages of poetry are out of the ordinary, but this is far less frequently the case in prose. The subject is more commonplace, and it is therefore less fitting in prose for a slave or a very young man to express himself in beautiful language on matters of too little importance. Even in prose, however, the appropriate diction may be either compact or amplified, but one must not be obviously composing; one must seem to be speaking in a natural and unstudied manner, for what is natural is convincing, what is studied is not. People distrust rhetorical tricks just as they distrust adulterated wines. The superiority of Theodorus over other actors was that he seemed to be speaking in a natural voice while theirs sounded artificial. Artifice is successful when the artist composes in the terms of current speech. Euripides does this and was the first to point the way.

Nouns and verbs are the elements of speech, and the different kinds of words were examined in the *Poetics*. There is very little occasion in prose to use strange words, compounds, or new coinages (we shall state later where they can be used), and the reason has already been stated: they make the language more elevated and unusual than is appropriate. Only current words, the proper names of things, and metaphors are to be used in prose, as is indicated by the fact that

[1] Nouns here include adjectives as in *Poetics* 20. By "nouns and verbs" Aristotle usually means words generally.

everybody uses only these. Everybody does use metaphors, the proper names of things, and current words in conversation, so that the language of a good writer must have an element of strangeness, but this must not obtrude, and he should be clear, for lucidity is the peculiar excellence of prose. Among nouns, homonyms are useful to the Sophists who trick people by means of them, as synonyms are useful to the poet.[2] By words which are both current and synonymous I mean, for example, "to travel" and "to journey"; both of these are current, and they are synonymous.

1405 a

The Metaphor

The nature of each of these kinds of words has already, as I said, been discussed in the *Poetics;* so have the different kinds of metaphor, and the extreme importance of metaphor in both prose and verse. One should the more carefully apply oneself to the study of metaphor in prose because prose has fewer aids than poetry. The metaphor is lucid, pleasing, and strange, and has all these qualities to a high degree; moreover, one cannot learn its use from anyone else. Both metaphors and epithets must be appropriate, and they will be appropriate if they point to a proportional likeness;[3] if they do not, they are inappropriate, for juxtaposition makes contradiction also more obvious.

Think of it this way: as a purple cloak is to youth, so to old age is—what? The same garment is obviously unsuitable. If you want to flatter your subject, you must derive your metaphor from the nobler things in the same genus; if you want to censure, from the worse. For example, since opposites belong to the same genus, you can say that one who is begging is praying, or that one who is praying is begging, for both are

[2] Aristotle adopts from Plato the derogatory meaning of the word Sophist. Homonyms are useful to him because they enable him to confuse his audience by substituting one for the other. Synonyms are useful to the poet because he can use them for ornamentation.

[3] For the meaning of "proportion" in connection with metaphors see *Poetics* 21 and note 2.

species of the genus asking. Iphicrates called Callias an alms collector instead of a torchbearer. Callias replied that Iphicrates was no initiate; if he were, he would not have called him an alms collector but a torchbearer.[4] Both titles concern the service of a god, but the second is honorable, which the first is not. Actors have been called flatterers of Dionysus, whereas they call themselves artists. Both are metaphors,[5] but the first is a term of abuse, and the second quite the contrary. Pirates call themselves purveyors; you can say that a wrongdoer has erred, or that one who has erred has done wrong, that a thief has taken something or that he has stolen it. When the Telephus of Euripides speaks of "lording it over the oar, and, landing in Mysia . . ," the expression "lording over" is inappropriate because it is too grand for the occasion, and the artifice is obvious. Then again the fault may lie in the actual sound of the syllables if it is unpleasing, as when Dionysius, whom they called the Brazen, speaks of poetry in his elegiacs as "the screeching of Calliope." Both screeches and poetry are sounds, and hence the metaphor, but it is a bad one, because screeches refer to sounds without meaning.

The metaphor must not be farfetched when we give names to things that have none by transference from things closely akin and similar to them in kind, and the kinship must be clear as soon as uttered, as in the well-known riddle: "I saw a man gluing bronze on another man with fire," for the process of cupping has no name, and both gluing and cupping are a kind of applying one thing to another, and so the word gluing was used of the application of the cupping glass.[6] Good metaphors can usually be made from successful riddles, for metaphors are a kind of riddle, and the transference of the word has then been successful.

1405 b

[4] The term δᾳδοῦχος (torchbearer) was the title of an honorable and usually hereditary office connected with the mysteries of Demeter, whereas the rarer word μητραγύρτης means a begging priest.

[5] If "artist" is a metaphor it means that Aristotle does not recognize acting as a true "art" (τέχνη).

[6] The same illustration is used in the *Poetics* 22.

A metaphor should also be derived from beautiful words. Now the beauty or ugliness of a word lies, as Licymnius says, in its sound or its meaning. There is, however, a third factor which disproves the contention of the Sophist Bryson who said that there is no such thing as bad language, for if the meaning is the same it makes no difference whether we use this word or that. This is not true. One word may be more current than the other, represent the object better, or be more apt to bring the thing vividly before our eyes. Words do not mean the same thing in quite the same way, so that one word must be considered more beautiful or ugly than the other. Both words may represent the same beautiful or ugly reality, but not qua beautiful or ugly, or at least not to the same degree. Metaphors should therefore be made from words that are beautiful in sound, in meaning, or by association to the eye or some other sense. "Rosy-fingered dawn," for example, is better than "purple-fingered," and "red-fingered" is even worse.

Importance of Words

Epithets, too, can add something, emphasize the worse or shameful side of things, or their better aspect. Orestes, for example, can be called a matricide, or the avenger of his father. A victor in a mule race asked Simonides to write an ode for a small fee; the poet refused indignantly, saying he would not write an ode to "half-donkeys," but, when an adequate fee had been offered, he wrote the poem beginning: "Hail, daughters of storm-footed steeds . . . ," but they were the daughters of donkeys, too. The same is true of the use of diminutives which minimize both the good and the bad. Aristophanes uses them in jest, and in the *Babylonians* he uses diminutives of gold, cloak, insult, and disease. Yet we should be careful and not go too far in the use of either epithets or diminutives.

III

Causes of Frigidity

Frigidity can result from the diction [1] in four ways. It can be due to the use of compounds, as when Lycophron speaks of "the multifaced sky of the mighty-peaked earth" and "the narrow-pathed beach," or Gorgias uses the expressions "a Muse-beggared flatterer" and "oath-observing" and "oath-foresworn." We find in Alcidamas "a soul filled with anger and a fire-colored face," and "he thought their eagerness to be end-attaining," and "end-attaining was the persuasion of his speech," and "the azure-colored floor of the ocean." All these compounds are felt to be poetical.

1406 a

That is one cause of frigidity. Another cause is the use of strange words, as when Lycophron calls Xerxes "a hugeous man," Sciron "a bale of a man," or when Alcidamas talks of the "play" of poetry, "the recklessness of nature," or of a man "whetted by the unadulterated anger of his mind."

The third cause of frigidity is the use of long, untimely, or too frequent epithets. A poet may speak of "white milk," but this is less appropriate in prose where, moreover, superfluous epithets betray artifice and make the effort at composition obvious. The effort itself is justified, for one must make use of these devices; they lift the diction out of the ordinary and give it an element of strangeness; but one must aim at moderation, for the excessive use of them is a worse evil than to speak at random, which is merely not good. Excess is here the cause of Alcidamas' frigidity: with him the epithets are not a seasoning, they are the whole dish. His epithets are too crowded, too grand, and too blatant: he cannot say "sweat" without saying "damp sweat"; he does not speak of going to the Isthmian games but to the "great assemblage of the Isthmian games"; he must needs speak of "those ruling monarchs of our cities, the laws"; instead of saying "in a race" he

1 For *lexis* see ch. 1, note 3.

speaks of "the racing impulse of the soul." [2] He does not say "museum" but talks of "having received the museum of nature" and of "the scowling thought of the mind"; he cannot say one who grants a favor, but "a popular favor," and speaks of one who is "a manager of pleasure for his hearers," of a man covering his nakedness not "with branches" but with "the branches of the forest"; moreover, he makes him cover not his body but "the shame of his body." When he speaks of "desire, the arch-mimicker of the soul," he uses an epithet which is also a compound, so that the whole phrase becomes poetry as does this other phrase of his: "vice transgressing the frontiers of perversity." Such inappropriately poetic language is both ridiculous and frigid; its verbosity also makes it obscure; the accumulation of words which add nothing to the sense beclouds what lucidity there is. Compound words are commonly used when certain things lack a name and their formation is simple, like the word "pastime," but it is poetical to use them frequently. For this reason compound words are most useful in dithyrambic poetry which is full of sound; rare words suit the epic which is dignified and proud, whereas metaphor is used in iambics, which, as I have said, poets now employ.

1406 b

The fourth kind of frigidity is in the use of metaphors. Metaphors can be inappropriate either because they are ludicrous (comic poets use metaphors, too) or because they are too solemn and tragic. They are obscure when they are too far-fetched, like Gorgias' "pale and bloodless events" or his "shamefully you sowed, evil was your harvest," for these are too poetical. Alcidamas again called philosophy "a rampart against the laws," and the *Odyssey* "a beautiful mirror of

[2] This and most of the other examples which follow to illustrate Alcidamas' excessive use of ornamental epithets are just as obscure in the Greek as they are in translation, for we do not have the contexts. The first presumably refers to someone running (and winning?) a race; what the reference to the museum of nature means we can only guess: museum meant originally a temple of the muses, then any place where the arts were practiced, including study. And we cannot even guess at the meaning of the description of desire.

human life," and he speaks of "bringing such a plaything to poetry." All these fail to carry conviction, for the reasons stated. Then there is the story of the swallow flying over Gorgias and letting its droppings fall on him, and he exclaimed in the best tragic style: "Shame on you, Philomela"—for what was natural for a bird was shameful for a maiden. So he reproached her by naming her as she used to be, not as she now was.[3]

IV

Similes

A simile is also a metaphor, and there is little difference between them. When Homer says of Achilles: "He leapt like a lion," it is a simile; but when he says "a lion he leapt," it is a metaphor, for he calls Achilles a lion by transference because both are brave. The simile is useful in prose also, but rarely, for it is a poetical device. Similes should be used in the same way as metaphors since they are metaphors with the difference we have noted. The following are examples of similes. Androtion said of Idreus that he was like a puppy let off the leash, for they attack one and bite, and Idreus was dangerous when released from prison. Theodamas said that Archidamus was like Euxenus without his knowledge of geometry; this was a metaphor of proportion, for Euxenus will be equal to Archidamus with knowledge of geometry added.[1] Plato, in the *Republic*, says that those who strip corpses on the battlefield are like dogs who snap at the stones that are thrown at them

[3] We should agree with Aristotle that Gorgias' reference to Philomela, who in legend was changed into a swallow, is frigid. We should also condemn most of his other examples, but the *Odyssey* as a mirror of human life rather appeals to us, except that by this time it is a cliché.

[1] Aristotle's explanation of these humorous similes seems a trifle ponderous. Presumably Archidamus thought of himself as a geometer, and perhaps Euxenus was little else, but I find it hard to reduce this to any proportional metaphor of the a is to b as c is to d kind. The references to the *Republic* are 5.469d; 6.488 (the famous parable of the ship of state) and 10.601b.

but ignore the man who throws them. Then there is his simile which compares the people to a strong but rather deaf ship-owner, and his saying that the verses of poets are like youths without true beauty: when the bloom of youth fades or the

1407 a meters are broken up, both are quite different. Pericles said that the Samians were like children who weep while they accept tidbits; he also compared the Boeotians to holm oaks which destroyed each other, because they were always fighting among themselves. Demosthenes compared the people to sea-sick passengers on a ship. Democrates compared politicians to nurses who gulp down the morsels of food themselves and rub the baby's lips with their spittle. Antisthenes said that Cephisodotus, who was very thin, was like incense: both delighted people by disappearing.

All these comparisons can be expressed either as similes or metaphors; all those that are successful when expressed as metaphors will also make similes, and all similes become metaphors when the explanation is omitted. The proportional metaphor must always be reversible as between two things which belong to the same genus. For example, if the cup can be said to be the shield of Dionysus, then the shield can be called the cup of Ares.[2]

V

Five Requirements of Style

These are the elements that go to make speech. The first principle of style is to write good Greek. For this five things are necessary, and the first is the proper use of connectives.[1]

[2] See ch. 1, note 5. Demetrius *On Style* (79) rightly corrects Aristotle: "Not all analogies, however, provide a metaphor that is reversible. The poet (Homer) could call the lower slopes of Ida the foot of the mountain, but he could not call a man's foot his slope."

[1] In Greek the logical connection between clauses, as also between sentences, is always expressed by conjunctions or connective particles unless deliberately omitted by a conscious figure of speech, which is hyperbaton. When Aristotle thus speaks of the proper use of connectives, he includes under this head the proper use of subordinate clauses and

These should correspond according to their nature, which requires some to precede, others to follow. In some cases this is obviously necessary: μέν used with an article or a pronoun clearly demands that a δέ should follow. The second particle should come while the first is still in the reader's mind; they should not be too far apart, nor should another connective introduce a further subordinate clause before the required connection is made, for this is rarely appropriate. In the sentence: "And I, after he had told me, for Cleon came begging and demanding it, started out with them," a number of connectives are inserted before the essential connection is made; when too many connections come before the main verb "started out," the result is obscure.

The first requirement of good Greek, then, is the proper use of connectives. The second is the use of specific rather than general terms. The third requirement is to avoid ambiguity, unless indeed the ambiguity is deliberately sought, as it is by those who pretend they have something to say when they have not. Such people usually say it in verse, like Empedocles. Elaborate circumlocutions deceive people who are impressed, as most people are impressed, by prophecies, so that they assent to ambiguous oracles like: "If Croesus crosses the river Halys, he will destroy a mighty kingdom." [2] A prophecy is less likely to be mistaken if it is expressed in general terms, and for this reason prophets use generic rather than specific language. A man is much more likely to guess right in playing odd and even than if he has to guess exact numbers; it is easier to foretell an event if one does not have to say when it will happen, and this is why oracle-mongers never add

1407 b

their relationship to each other. In English and most modern languages such connectives are omitted and the logical connection only expressed when important. Any attempt to translate the Greek particles would be intolerably labored and prolix. Among the most common of Greek particles is μέν, used in the first, followed by δέ in the second member of an antithesis, even where the antithesis is of the mildest. So μέν generally requires an answering δέ, as Aristotle notes in the next sentence.

[2] The story is well known; it was his own kingdom which Croesus destroyed, Herodotus 1.53.

the "when." All these ambiguities are much the same and should be avoided, unless there is some such reason for them.

The fourth requirement is to follow Protagoras' proper distinctions of gender. These must correspond, as in

ἡ δ' ἐλθοῦσα καὶ διαλεχθεῖσα ᾤχετο.

The fifth requirement is the correct use of singular and plural for many, few or one, as, for example:

οἱ δ' ἐλθόντες ἔτυπτόν με.[3]

In general, what we write should be easy to read and easy to speak, which comes to the same thing. This will not be so if we use too many connectives (and subordinate clauses), or if our sentences are hard to punctuate, like those of Heraclitus. It is a difficult task to insert the right punctuation in his work, for it is often far from clear whether a certain word is to be taken with what precedes or with what follows, as when he said at the beginning of his work, "Reason being such always men fail to understand," where it is not clear whether "always" should be taken with the preceding or the following words.[4]

Moreover a solecism results when words do not properly correspond, as when two words are joined with another which does not apply to both: one may speak of "perceiving" both a noise and a color, but not of "seeing" them. To avoid obscurity, the sense of the main clause should be clear before a num-

---

[3] The point of the first example is that the participles ἐλθοῦσα and διαλεχθεῖσα are in the feminine, agreeing with the feminine subject: "Having come and conversed, she went away." So in the last example, the participle ἐλθόντες is masculine plural and the verb ἔτυπτον is in the plural, agreeing with the plural subject: "Having come, they were beating me."

[4] E. M. Cope (An Introduction to Aristotle's Rhetoric, London, 1867, p. 294) has an attractive note on this section: "No reader of Aristotle, who has suffered from his inattention to this very same essential of perspicuous writing, can fail to be amused with the naiveté and happy unconsciousness which he here shows in laying down a rule for others which he is constantly violating himself . . . it is indeed a grave case of Satan rebuking sin."

ber of other things are inserted. It is wrong to say "I was intending, after speaking to him and this and that and so and
so, to leave" instead of "I was intending to leave after talking
to him, and then so and so happened."

VI

A Weighty Style

The following devices contribute to a weighty style: [1] use
the descriptive definition instead of the noun; say, for example, "a two-dimensional figure equidistant from the center"
instead of "circle," whereas conciseness is obtained by using
the noun instead of the definition. (The same can be done in
referring to something ugly or unseemly: use the definition if
the noun is unseemly, or, if the definition is unseemly, use the
noun.) Use metaphors as illustrations, and add epithets, so
long as the poetical is avoided. You can also use the plural, as
the poets do: they speak of "the harbors of Achaia," though
there is only one, and of "these many-leaved folds of the writing tablet." Do not run things together but express each point
separately, as in "this wife of mine" instead of "my wife,"
which you will say if you want to be concise. Use a full com-
plement of connectives; conciseness omits them, though not
to the point of asyndeton; one can say either πορευθεὶς καὶ   1408 a
διαλεχθείς or πορευθεὶς διελέχθην.[2] Antimachus' advice is also useful, namely, to describe an object by the qualities it does not
possess, as he does in his description of Teumessus which be-

---

[1] Aristotle is not *advising* a weighty or "bulky" style, but as usual
dispassionately analyzing the methods by which it can be obtained if
desired. Indeed, it is hard to believe that he is not being ironical, as he
obviously is about Empedocles and the prophets in the previous chapter,
especially if we remember his remarks on Alcidamas in ch. 3.

[2] The first phrase has two participles connected by καί (and): "having
walked and having conversed," while in the second one of the participles
is replaced by a finite verb, so that the connective is dropped and the
expression more concise.

gins: "There is a little wind-swept hill . . . ." This kind of description can be prolonged indefinitely. This method of describing things negatively can be used of good qualities or bad, whichever is useful at the time. Poets coin expressions of this kind, such as "stringless" and "lyreless" music, and they add epithets to describe qualities that are lacking. This is attractive in metaphors of proportion, as to say that the trumpet utters "a lyreless song."

VII

Appropriateness

The diction will be appropriate if it expresses emotion and character, and is in keeping with the subject matter.[1] "In keeping" means that a weighty subject is not expressed in trivial language or a trivial subject in solemn language, or a common word adorned with ornamental epithets. Otherwise the result will be comic. It is so in the poetry of Cleophon, for some of his expressions are as absurd as if he had spoken of an "august fig." The diction will express the appropriate emotion if insolence is described in the language of anger, impious and ugly deeds are related with indignation and reluctance, praiseworthy deeds with admiration, pitiful things described with humility, and so on. Appropriate language makes the matter convincing; those who hear it are misled into thinking that what the speaker says is true because he expresses the emotions one would feel under those circumstances, and so they think the facts are as the speaker tells them, even if they are not. An audience always shares the feelings of a passionate speaker, even when there is nothing in what he says. That is why so many orators tumultuously overwhelm their audiences with their uproar.

The language will be in character if it displays the peculi-

---

[1] "Diction" in all ancient critics includes the choice of words which are in character and express the right emotion and passion, as well as the use of metaphor.

arities which are consistent with, and appropriate to, every group and every disposition. By group I mean age group, i.e., whether the person who is speaking is a child, a mature man, or an old man, or whether the speaker is a man or a woman, a Spartan or a Thessalian; by disposition I mean that which gives a certain flavor to an individual's life, although not every disposition does this. If then the language used is appropriate to the disposition as well as to the group, it will be in character: a peasant does not say the same things, nor say them in the same way, as an educated man. An audience is also affected by a device which speech writers use to excess, namely, such phrases as "who is not aware that" or "everybody knows." Such expressions shame the hearer into agreeing, for fear that he lacks the knowledge everyone else has.

There is a right and a wrong time to use all these kinds of devices. There is also a common remedy for every exaggerated use of them, and it is well known: the speaker reproves himself for it in advance; then what he says is thought to be true, since he knows what he is doing. Not all similar devices should be used at once if the hearer is to remain unsuspicious. For example, if your words are harsh, your voice, features, and all that goes with them should not be harsh to the same degree, otherwise every trick is seen for what it is, but if you use one without the other, the same effect can be obtained without arousing suspicion. However, harsh words spoken in a soft voice, or soft words in a harsh voice, carry no conviction.

1408 b

Compound words, numerous epithets, and strange words are especially appropriate in passionate speeches. An angry man can be forgiven for saying that a certain evil is "heaven-high" or "prodigious." When a speaker has taken hold of his audience and they are carried away by admiration, hatred, anger, or sympathy, he can use words of that kind, as Isocrates does at the end of his *Panegyric*, where we find such expressions as "repute and remembrance" and "those who durst contemplate." Men speak like that under the stress of strong emotions, and their audience will tolerate it when it has reached a similar emotional pitch. For this reason such expressions are suitable in poetry, for poetry is a kind of frenzy.[2] They must then be used in this way, or else ironically, as Gorgias did, and Plato in the *Phaedrus*.

VIII

Prose Rhythm

In form, prose should not be metrical, nor should it be without rhythm. Metrical prose is unconvincing because it betrays artifice; it also distracts the hearer who is led to look for the recurrence of a similar metrical pattern. So children forestall the answer to the herald's question, "Whom does this freed slave choose as his patron?" by shouting "Cleon." [1] On the other hand, prose without rhythm is formless, and it should have form, but not meter. The indefinite and formless is displeasing and cannot be known. All things are limited by number, and rhythm is the number which limits the shape of prose (meter, too, is a subdivision of rhythm). Prose then must have rhythm but not meter, for if it has meter it will be a poem. Nor should this rhythm be precise; it must only, that is, be carried to a certain point.

[2] The actual word used by Aristotle is ἔνθεον, which means "possessed by a god." The translation "inspired" would give quite the wrong idea. What Aristotle obviously has in mind is that poetry has *pathos*, a high emotional pitch. This is a natural meaning of the word, as of its cognate *enthousiasmos* and it is the only meaning that makes sense in this context. Cp. Croissant (note 13 in Introduction), pp. 43-46 and *passim*. The Platonic reference which follows is to *Phaedrus* 241d where the irony is quite explicit, though later critics like Dionysius ignored it.

[1] A freedman, not possessing citizen rights, needed a patron among the citizens. Presumably in his day Cleon, who posed as the champion of the people and of the underdog, was ready to give protection to new freedmen, and we may well believe that many were glad to avail themselves of such a powerful protector. Hence the almost inevitable answer to the herald's question was "Cleon," so much so that the children in the market place could anticipate it.

As for different rhythms,[2] the heroic has dignity, but it is lacking in the cadence of prose; the iambic is the rhythm of ordinary conversation. More iambics occur spontaneously in prose than any other meter, but prose should have dignity and stir an audience. The trochee is too reminiscent of the vulgar cordax dance; the trochaic tetrameter shows this, for it is a tripping measure. That leaves the paeon which has been used in prose since Thrasymachus, but its nature has not been explained.

The paeon is a third rhythm closely related to the others we mentioned; its two parts are in the ratio of three to two, whereas the others have a ratio of one to one, or two to one. Now the ratio of the paeon, one and a half to one, is closely connected to both these other ratios. These must be rejected for the reasons mentioned, and also because they are more obviously metrical, and so the paeon is to be preferred. Unlike the others it is not the basis of a well-known metrical system, so that it will more easily escape notice. Only one kind of paeon is in use at present, at the beginning of a clause, but the end should be different from the beginning. There are two opposite kinds of paeon: one of these is suited to the beginning of a clause, and is now so used; it consists of a long syllable followed by three shorts, e.g., Δαλογενὲς εἴτε Λυκίαν ("O thou born in Delos or maybe Lycia . . .") and χρυσεοκόμα Ἕκατε παῖ Διός ("Golden-haired far-shooter, son of Zeus"). The other paeon, on the contrary, consists of three shorts followed by a long syllable, as in μετὰ δὲ γᾶν ὕδατα τ' ὠκεανὸν ἠψάνισε νύξ ("after the earth and the waters, the night darkened the ocean").[3]

---

[2] The heroic meter includes the dactyl (— ∪ ∪) and the spondee (— —). In these meters the two parts are in the ratio of 1 to 1 (two shorts being the equivalent of one long); the iambic (∪ —), on the other hand, and the trochee (— ∪) have their parts in the ratio of 1 to 2 or 2 to 1. The paeon (— ∪ ∪ ∪ or ∪ ∪ ∪ —) has its parts in the ratio of 2 to 3 or 3 to 2.

[3] The examples are quoted in Greek because it is the rhythm of the Greek words which is relevant. The translation is added for the con-

This makes a good ending, for a short syllable is incomplete
and gives an impression of amputation at the end. The end of
a sentence should be marked off by a long syllable; it should
be indicated by the rhythm, not merely by the copyist or by a
special mark in the text. We have now established that prose
should not be without rhythm but should be rhythmical, what
rhythms are best, and what their nature is.

IX

Sentence Structure: the Period

There are two styles of composition or word arrangement:
the loose or strung-along style in which the clauses are united
only by the connectives, like the preludes in dithyrambs,[1] and
the periodic style which turns back upon itself like the antistrophes of the old poets. The strung-along style is the older:
"The following is the published record of the investigations
of Herodotus of Thurii." Everybody used to write like that,
but nowadays few people use the strung-along style, which,
as the name indicates, has no natural ending to its sentences
unless the subject matter runs out. It is unpleasing because it
is endless, and people always like to have an end in sight.
When runners come to the finishing post, they are exhausted
and out of breath, but they do not give way before because
they see the goal ahead of them.

Such then is the strung-along style, but the style that turns
back upon itself expresses itself in periods, that is, in sentences
which have a beginning and an end of their own, and a length
1409 b   that can be seen as a whole. This style is pleasing and easy to
grasp—pleasing because it is the opposite of shapeless and because the hearer feels at any moment that he has grasped
something and that something has been completed for him.

---

venience of the reader but is, of course, irrelevant. The first two examples
begin with two paeons ($- \cup \cup \cup - \cup \cup \cup$), the third ends with one
paeon ($\cup \cup \cup -$).

1 For the dithyramb see *Poetics* 1, note 2.

To foresee nothing and accomplish nothing is unpleasant. The periodic style is also easy to learn because it is easy to remember, and it is easy to remember because it is limited by number, which of all things makes the strongest appeal to the memory. Everybody remembers verses more easily than a mere flow of words, for verses are measured by number. The period should come to an end at the same time as the thought, and not be cut off as in the iambic line of Sophocles:

> And this is Calydon, of Pelops' land . . .

for punctuation may give it a sense opposite to that intended, as in this case, if we divide the sentence here, namely, that Calydon is part of the Peloponnesus.[2]

A period may be composed of clauses or it may be simple. A period which consists of clauses should be a completed whole which falls into parts and is easy to speak in one breath. It should not depend on punctuation like the period just quoted. Each part of that period is a clause. A simple period consists of only one clause. Neither clauses nor periods should be either cut short or lengthy; if too short, they often make the reader stumble: he is pressing on to a longer measure of which he has a notion in his mind and is pulled up short as if he stumbled over an obstacle; if too long, they leave him behind, as those who, in a walking race, walk on beyond the turning point and leave their competitors behind them. A lengthy period tends to become a whole speech, as dithyrambic preludes tend to become whole poems. This leads to what Democritus of Chios ridiculed in Melanippides, that he wrote preludes instead of antistrophes:

> Harm he plans for himself, who plans to do harm to another,
> A prelude that is too long is a dreadful thing for a poet.[3]

---

[2] But this was not the case; in context the words read: "And this is Calydon, of Pelops' land the opposite shore. . . ."

[3] This is a witty adaptation of two lines of Hesiod: the first line is unchanged. The second line in Hesiod (*Works and Days* 266) went on to say that evil counsel was most evil to the counselor.

The same might be said of those whose clauses are too lengthy. Excessively brief clauses, on the other hand, do not make a period; they rush the reader headlong.

Antithesis

There are two kinds of clauses in the periodic style: those that merely divide a period and those that form an antithesis. A period like the following is merely divided: "I have often admired those who organize these great assemblies and those who have established the gymnastic contests." In the antithetic style, on the other hand, each clause is opposed to the other, or two contraries are linked with one verb, as in: "They benefited both those who had remained at home and those who had followed them; to the latter they secured more land than they had possessed at home, to the former they left land at home which was now adequate." "Remained" is here opposed to "followed" and "more" to "adequate." In "both for those who needed money and those who wished to enjoy it," enjoying is opposed to acquiring.[4] Then again: "It often happens in such cases that the wise fail and the fools succeed." "At once the prize of bravery was deemed to be theirs; a little later they acquired command of the sea." "By bridging the Hellespont and digging through Mount Athos, they sailed over the land and marched over the sea." [5] "Though citizens by birth, they were by law deprived of citizenship." "Some died a terrible death, others found a disgraceful safety." "As individuals we use barbarians as our servants, as citizens we tolerate many of our allies being enslaved." ". . . either to

1410 a

---

[4] The Greek of this last example is ὥστε καὶ τοῖς χρημάτων δεομένοις καὶ τοῖς ἀπολαῦσαι βουλομένοις, and he comments: ἀπόλαυσις κτήσει ἀντίκειται. But "acquiring" (κτῆσις) does not, strictly speaking, occur in the first term of the antithesis, which speaks of "needing" (δεομένοις). If we had the context the point would probably be clarified.

The antitheses can be rendered in translation. Most of the Greek illustrations, however, also have homoioteleuton. This is here irrelevant and is discussed separately below (ch. 9, note 6).

[5] The reference is to Xerxes' invasion of Greece in 480 B.C.

possess in life or to leave behind in death." Someone said in court against Peitholaus and Lycophron: "At home they used to sell you, now they have come to buy you." All these are examples of antithesis. This antithetic style is pleasing because contraries are easy to understand, the more so in juxtaposition, and also because the construction resembles a syllogism, for refutation consists of bringing contraries together.

Parisosis and Paromoiosis

Such then is the nature of antithesis. *Parisosis* occurs when clauses or phrases are of equal length; *paromoiosis,* when each of two clauses or phrases begins or ends with similar sounds. The similarities must occur at the beginning or the end; at the beginning the similarity lies in whole words; at the end it may be only in the last syllables, or in different inflections of the same word, or a word may be repeated. The following are examples [6] of paromoiosis at the beginning: ἀγρὸν γὰρ ἔλαβεν ἀργὸν παρ' αὐτοῦ ("he received from him uncultivated land"), and also: δωρητοί τ' ἐπέλοντο παραρρητοί τ' ἐπέεσσιν ("swayed by gifts, waylaid by words"). Paromoiosis at the end occurs in ᾠήθησαν αὐτὸν παιδίον τετοκέναι, ἀλλ' αὐτοῦ αἴτιον γεγονέναι ("they thought he was the father of a child, but that he was the cause

[6] The examples which follow are quoted in Greek because it is the sound of the Greek words that is relevant, not the meaning (though the translation is added after each example merely for the convenience of the reader). Of the two examples of paromoiosis or similarity of sound at the beginning of two clauses or phrases, the first is a fragment of Aristophanes, the second a quotation from Homer (*Iliad* 9.526), and an attempt is made to keep something of the jingle in the translation. The rest are examples of paromoiosis at the end of successive clauses, also called homoioteleuton; here we should remember that the Greeks did not know rhyme, so that similar endings did not recall verse to them. The meaning of the first example ("they thought he was the father . . .") is quite obscure and indeed the text is probably corrupt; a negative may possibly have fallen out in the first part. Its origin is unknown and so is that of the next two, though the meaning is clear: the play on χαλκός is that the adjective first refers to a bronze statue and then the noun refers to money.

of it"), and in ἐν πλείσταις δὲ φροντίσι καὶ ἐν ἐλαχίσταις ἔλπισι ("in very great anxieties and very little hope"). We have inflected forms of the same word in: ἄξιος δὲ σταθῆναι χαλκοῦς οὐκ ἄξιος ὢν χαλκοῦ ("worthy to stand in bronze but worth no money"); the same word occurs in: σὺ δ᾽ αὐτὸν καὶ ζῶντα ἔλεγες κακῶς καὶ νῦν γράφεις κακῶς, ("when he lived you spoke ill of him, and now you write ill of him"), and the same syllable only in

1410 b   τί ἂν ἔπαθες δεινόν, εἰ ἄνδρ᾽ εἶδες ἀργόν ("what terrible thing would you have suffered if you had seen an idle man?").

All three, antithesis, parisosis, and homoioteleuton may occur together, and the different ways to begin a period are all enumerated in the writings of Theodectes. There are also false antitheses, as in the line of Epicharmus: "At one time I was at their house, at one time I was with them." [7]

X

Happy Phrases

Now that we have defined the above, the next question is how felicitous [1] and successful sayings originate. Natural talent or technical training gives them utterance; our task in this investigation is to explain what they are. We must therefore discuss and enumerate them, taking as our starting point the fact that human nature delights in learning something with ease. Words express a meaning, and those words are the most pleasing which make us learn something. We know the current words, but not those that are rare.

---

[7] Each clause begins with τόκα. Demetrius *On Style* (24) uses the same example of a purely verbal antithesis and adds, "this was probably a jest at the expense of the rhetoricians," i.e., Epicharmus is ridiculing their excessive use of antithesis.

[1] The Greek word ἀστεῖος, which originally meant "of the city" as opposed to the country, is correctly translated *urbanus* by the Romans, but our own word "urbane" has different connotations. The word was later restricted to witticisms, but, as can be seen from the examples, this cannot be the exclusive meaning here. It means rather a happy phrase; it is translated by "felicitous."

We learn above all from metaphors. When Homer compares old age to wheat stubble,[2] he makes us realize and understand that both wheat stubble and old age belong to the genus of things that have lost their vigor. Poetic similes have the same effect, and, when they are good, the effect is felicitous. The simile, as I said before, is a metaphor with something added; it is less pleasing because it makes the point at greater length; it does not identify two things, and so the mind does not examine the relation.

Both the language and the reasoning behind it are necessarily felicitous if we learn something from them quickly. The obvious does not appeal to us much (by obvious I mean what is plain to everybody and requires no investigation), nor are we attracted by what we do not understand, but we are attracted by those things which we understand as soon as they are said or very soon afterwards, even though we had no knowledge of them before, for then there is a learning process or something very like it, but in the case of the obvious or the unintelligible there is no learning at any time. These, then, are the kinds of thoughts which have considerable appeal, as far as the content is concerned.

As for its expression, there is the form and there are the words. The form is attractive if there is an antithesis, as in "What to others was an all-embracing peace they considered to be war upon their own interests," [3] where peace forms an antithesis to war. The words appeal to us if there is a metaphor which must not be farfetched, for then it is difficult to grasp the whole idea, nor obvious, for then it does not affect us at all. Further, the words should bring things before our eyes; they must give an impression of things happening in the present, not in the future. These three things should be aimed at: metaphor, antithesis, and vividness.

---

2 *Odyssey* 14.213: "I think that, looking on the stubble, you will recognize my former strength. . . ."
3 Isocrates, *Philippus* 73.

Examples of Metaphors

There are four kinds of metaphor, and of these the metaphor from proportion (a : b : : c : d) is the most attractive, as when Pericles said that the loss of the city's youth during the war was as if the spring had been taken out of the year. Leptines, speaking of Sparta, said that they would not allow Athens to stand by while Greece lost one of its eyes.[4] When Chares was anxious to submit his accounts of the Olynthian war, Cephisodotus said angrily that he was trying to have his accounts examined while he had the people by the throat. The same orator, when advising the Athenians to go to Euboea and provision themselves there, said that the decree of Miltiades must go on this expedition.[5] When the Athenians had made a truce with Epidaurus and the cities along the coast, Iphicrates declared angrily that they had cut off their own supplies.[6] Peitholaus called the Paralos the cudgel of the people,[7] and Sestos the corn chest of the Peiraeus.[8] Pericles bade the Athenians conquer Aegina and remove the eyesore of the Peiraeus. Moirocles said he was no worse a rascal than a respectable citizen whom he named and who, he said, charged thirty-three per cent for his rascality while he himself charged only ten.[9] Then we have the iambic verse of

1411 a (margin)

---

[4] In the rest of this chapter, Aristotle gives over twenty more examples of metaphor. Some are striking, but several are quite obscure even in the Greek because they are quoted without context. An attempt is here made to translate them all, for the sake of completeness, but the nonspecialist reader may be well advised to proceed at once to the next chapter.

[5] The meaning is quite unknown.

[6] Presumably because they could not now attack those cities and plunder them.

[7] The Paralos was one of the two sacred galleys kept by the Athenians for ceremonial occasions. They were also used to carry official messages, or news of decrees of the people, or to carry prisoners. There is a pun here on the word ῥόπαλος (cudgel).

[8] Sestos, on the coast of the Dardanelles, commanded the corn route to the Black Sea.

[9] Perhaps both lent money at interest, but Moirocles was more notorious.

Anaxandrides on behalf of his daughters who were delaying marriage: "My maidens are defaulting on wedlock." Polyeuctes said of a certain Speusippus, who was liable to epileptic fits, that he could not keep still even when fastened by Fortune to the pillory of disease. Cephisodotus called the triremes decorated corn mills,[10] while the Cynic called the taverns the phiditia of Athens.[11]

Aision said that the Athenians had poured away their city into Sicily;[12] this is a metaphor and an example of vividness, and so is another expression of his: "so that Greece cried out," for this too is a kind of metaphor and makes us visualize things. Then again Cephisodotus bade the Athenians to be careful not to rush their meetings too often,[13] and Isocrates made a similar remark about those who rush to the national festivals. We find in the funeral oration[14] that it was fitting for Greece to cut her locks at the grave of those who died at Salamis, for her freedom was buried with their bravery. If he had said that it was fitting for Greece to weep as their bravery was buried with them, the expression would have been metaphorical and vivid, but "her freedom with their bravery" is a kind of antithesis as well. When Iphicrates said: "The path of my words lies through the midst of Chares' deeds," this is a proportional metaphor, and "through the midst" makes for vividness.[15] To say that one should call upon dangers to meet

1411 b

10 Athens had to import her corn, for which the fleet was all-important. Some also see a reference here to "grinding down" the allies.

11 The phiditia were the Spartan military messes where the Spartan men ate and lived. The Cynic is presumably Diogenes of Sinope, and he obviously meant that the Athenians spent as much time in the taverns as the Spartans in the phiditia, or, in Aristotelian terms: The taverns were to the Athenians what the phiditia were to the Spartans.

12 The reference must be to the disastrous Sicilian expedition of 415 B.C. described in the sixth and seventh books of Thucydides.

13 Literally: not to have too many συνδρομαί, which refers to tumultuous gatherings. The reference to Isocrates is *Philippus* 12.

14 Lysias 2.60.

15 Presumably words are to Iphicrates as deeds are to Chares, but the metaphor surely lies in the word path (ὁδός).

dangers is also a vivid metaphor. Lycoleon, speaking in defense of Chabrias, said: "feeling no shame before this suppliant on his behalf, this image in bronze"; here the metaphor depends on the particular circumstances of the moment and is not of universal validity, but it is vivid, for Chabrias is in danger, and the inanimate statue is represented as alive to pray for him, itself a memorial of the benefits he had conferred upon the state.[16] The phrase "studying narrow-mindedness in every way" is also a metaphor, because studying is a kind of increasing.[17] So also is the saying that "the god has kindled intelligence, a light in the soul," for both intelligence and light make things clear. "We do not end our wars, we delay them" [18] is a metaphor because both delay and the kind of peace referred to are forms of putting things off. Or again, to say of a peaceful settlement, "it is a far finer trophy than those set up in war, as the latter celebrate mere incidents or a single success, whereas treaties celebrate the end of the whole war," is a metaphor, for both are tokens of victory. Also the saying: "Cities give a full account of themselves before the reprobation of men," for to give an account of oneself is a kind of penalty.

XI

The Active Metaphor

We have seen that felicitous sayings result from the use of a proportional metaphor and from bringing things vividly before the eyes of the audience. We must now say what we mean by "before the eyes" and how this is achieved. It is an

16 There was a statue of the Athenian general Chabrias in the market place, representing him kneeling, and we may suppose that Lycoleon points to it. This is an "animate" metaphor of the kind explained in the next chapter.

17 The phrase occurs in Isocrates, *Panegyricus* 151. As studying leads one to increase some talent, studying is considered as a species of the genus increase. But the expression is rather a paradox than a metaphor.

18 Also from *Panegyricus* (172) and so is the next quotation (180).

effect produced by words which refer to things in action: to say, for example, that a good man is "foursquare" is a metaphor, for both the man and the square are complete and perfect, but it does not indicate action; on the other hand, to speak of man's prime as "in full bloom" does express activity. So does the description of Philip as "ranging over Greece," or the line of Euripides saying that the Greeks were "darting forward," for darting is a metaphor which indicates action. Homer frequently uses this device when he speaks metaphorically of inanimate things as animated; these expressions are attractive because they represent things as acting. He says: "Once more the shameless rock rolled down into the plain," he speaks of an arrow "flying" or "eager to fly," of spears "standing fast in the ground, though longing to feed on his flesh," and "the spear point eagerly piercing his chest." In all these cases, things are represented as alive and in action. Shamelessness, eagerness, and the rest imply living and acting, and he joins these attributes to the nouns by means of proportional metaphor. The rock is to Sisyphus as a shameless torturer is to his victim. Homer similarly endows the inanimate with life in his famous similes, as when he speaks of "arched, crested" waves beating on the shore.[1] He makes everything live and move, and vividness implies movement.

1412 a

As I said before, metaphor must be by transference from things that are related, but not obviously so, as it is a sign of sound intuition in a philosopher to see similarities between things that are far apart. Archytas said that an arbitrator was the same as an altar, as the victims of wrongdoing seek refuge with both. Or one might say that an anchor and a hook are the same; indeed they are the same, except that one acts from above and the other from below. And the expression "putting cities on a level" also refers to a similarity between things far apart; the equalization of a surface and of powers.

---

[1] The reference to Philip of Macedon as "ranging over Greece" is from Isocrates' *Philippus* 127. The Homeric expressions will be found in *Odyssey* 11.598 (the stone of Sisyphus) and *Iliad* 13.587; 4.126; 11.574; and 13.799.

Most felicitous sayings rely on metaphor and on a capacity to deceive beforehand. We have even more obviously learned something if things are the opposite of what we thought they were, and the mind seems to say to itself: "How true; I was mistaken." Felicitous epigrammatic statements say one thing and mean another, as in Stesichorus' threat: "Your grasshoppers will sing to themselves from the ground." [2] Good riddles delight us for the same reason, for we learn something from them, and they are in the form of metaphors. This is what Theodorus says, that "one should say something new," and this happens when, as he puts it, things are different from what we expected, when, that is, they are paradoxical, as when words are miscoined in jest, or where the joke depends on the change of one letter. All this is a kind of deception which is also found in verse, for it is not what the hearer expected: "He marched, and on his feet his—chilblains," where one expected sandals. But the point must be clear at once.

Examples of Wit

Jokes depending on one letter also produce a different meaning, namely, that of the changed word, as when Theodorus said to Nicon the lyre player, Θράττει, for he pretends to mean θράττει σε, but this is a deception and he means something else.[3] This is pleasant to those in the know, but it will not seem felicitous if one does not know that Nicon was a Thracian. So with the expression βούλει αὐτὸν πέρσαι.[4] However, both meanings must be appropriate. So with felicitous sayings generally, as, for example, to say to the Athenians that their rule (ἀρχή) over the sea was not the beginning (ἀρχή) of their

1412 b

---

[2] This is a favorite of later critics. The meaning is, of course, "I shall raze your city to the ground."

[3] The point of the pun is obscure. One expects Theodorus, says Aristotle, to say "(something) troubles you"; the secondary meaning may, as has been suggested, be Θρᾷττ' εἶ, you are a Thracian slave girl (or no better than one).

[4] Here some play is presumably intended on πέρσαι (to destroy) and Πέρσαι (Persians), but the point of it is lost.

misfortunes, or, as Isocrates did, that their city's empire (ἀρχή) was the beginning of their misfortunes,[5] for in neither case is the meaning what was expected. There is nothing clever in saying that ἀρχή is ἀρχή (in the same sense), but this is not what he says for he uses the word differently, in a different sense in the negative clause. In all such cases the word should be appropriately used as a homonym or metaphorically to obtain a good result, as in Anaschetos is not tolerable (ἀνασχετός),[6] or "you should not be more of a stranger than a stranger," that is, more than you should be, which means the same thing; or again, "a stranger should not always remain a stranger" where the word is again used in a different sense. The same is true of the much-praised line of Anaxandrides, καλόν γ' ἀποθανεῖν πρὶν θανάτου δρᾶν ἄξιον ("worthy it is to die before being worthy of death"), for this is the same as saying that it is a worthy thing to die before one has earned death, or that it is worthy to die before one deserves death, i.e., before doing anything which deserves the death penalty.[7]

In all these sayings the form of expression is the same, but their success is in direct proportion to their brevity and their antithetic form; and the reason is that we learn more easily from an antithesis, and more quickly from conciseness. What is said should always refer to a particular person, or be well expressed, if it is to strike us as true but not obvious. The ideas can be expressed separately, "one should die without sin," but there is nothing felicitous in that, any more than in "a worthy man should wed a worthy woman"; but if one combines the two meanings of worthy, "it is worthy to die without being worthy of death," that is felicitous. The more an expression contains, the more felicitous it is, as when the words are

[5] All these are straightforward puns on the various meanings of ἀρχή, namely rule, empire, or beginning. The reference to Isocrates is *On the Peace* 101.

[6] A man called Anaschetos is not *anaschetos* (bearable or tolerable). Some editors translate: "There is no bearing Baring."

[7] Here the play is on the word ἄξιος, worthy or deserving of.

metaphorical, when the metaphor is of the better kind, when there is antithesis, and parisosis, and also vividness.

Similes, as I have said above, are a kind of metaphor. Like the proportional metaphor, they always refer to two things, as 1413 a we said, the shield is the cup of Ares, or the bow is a stringless lyre. Such comparisons are more than a simple transference, like calling the bow a lyre or the shield a goblet. Comparisons can be made in this simpler way, as when a flute player is compared to an ape (in posture) or a shortsighted man to a sputtering lamp, for both the flame and the eye contract; but the best image involves a metaphor, for we can describe the shield as the goblet of Ares, or a ruin as the tatters of a house. Thrasymachus called Niceratus a Philoctetes bitten by Pratys when he saw him defeated by Pratys in a rhapsody contest, his hair unkempt and his clothes dirty. Poets are hissed off the stage if their metaphors are bad, but good metaphors are much applauded, when there is a true correspondence between the terms.

All such sayings as "He stood on legs as twisted as parsley," or "He fought like Philammon at the punching bag," are similes, and we have already said often enough that similes are metaphors.

Proverbs

Proverbs, too, are metaphors with transference from species to species of the same genus. When a man brings something home which he thinks will benefit him, and is then hurt by it, he says it is a case of the Carpathian and the hare, for both have suffered unexpected injury.

We have now dealt fairly adequately with felicitous sayings, their origin, the cause and reason of their success.

Hyperboles

Successful hyperboles are also metaphors, as when it was said of a man with a black eye: "You'd take him for a basket of mulberries," a black eye, too, being purple, and the quantity of mulberries provides the exaggeration. Any comparison can become a hyperbole if expressed in a certain way. The simile, "like Philammon at the punching bag," becomes a hyperbole if you say: "You'd have thought he was Philammon at the punching bag," and "He stood on legs twisted like parsley" can be put hyperbolically: "His legs were so twisted that you'd think he was standing on parsley." There is something adolescent about hyperboles, for they express things violently: "Not if her gifts were as numerous as grains of sand or dust would I marry the daughter of Agamemnon, not if she rivaled the golden Aphrodite in beauty, or Athena in her handiwork." [8] The Attic orators are very partial to hyperbole; its vehemence, however, does not suit men of mature years.

1413 b

XII

Variations in Style

It should be observed that every type of rhetoric requires a different style. That of written prose is different from that of actual debate, and one needs to know both, and, further, forensic and political debates require different styles. In speaking, it is a question of talking good Greek, in writing it is a question of not having to remain silent when one has something to communicate, which is the fate of those who cannot write. Written style is the more precise, whereas the style of debate relies more on delivery. There are two kinds of delivery: that which expresses character,[1] and the passionate; that is why actors are always looking for plays of the one kind or the other, and the poets look for those kinds of actor. There are, however, plays in circulation which are better read, like those of Chaeremon, who is as precise as a professional speechwriter, and the poems of Licymnius among the writers of dithyrambs. When they are compared, written work sounds thin in actual debate, while the speeches of orators sound well when delivered but seem amateurish when read. The reason is

[8] The words are spoken by Achilles in *Iliad* 9.385, 387-90. Aristotle here quotes correctly but omits two lines.

[1] For the meaning of character or *éthos* here see *Poetics* 24, note 2.

that they are suited to debate, and that those passages which
rely on delivery cannot be effective without it and seem silly,
with their frequent asyndeta and repetitions which are rightly
deprecated in written work, but frequently used even by professional orators, for they are histrionic.

One must, however, introduce variations in repetition, and
these pave the way for variations in delivery: "This is the man
who robbed you, the man who deceived you, the man who in
the end tried to betray you." The actor Philemon did this in
acting *The Mad Old Man* of Anaxandrides, where he had to
repeat the names "Rhadamanthys and Palamedes" several
times, and also when repeating the pronoun "I" in the pro-
logue to *The Pious Men*. Without such variations the delivery
becomes stiff and awkward.

Asyndeton

The same is true of asyndeta like "I came, I met him, I en-
treated": they require an actor's delivery; one must not say
the same thing in the same manner and the same tone. Asyndeton has a peculiar effect: it seems to say many things at the
same time. Connectives tie up many things into one; when
they are withdrawn the opposite result is obviously achieved
and one thing becomes many; it has, therefore, an effect of
amplification as in "I came, I spoke with him, I begged him."
The speaker seems to look over many things, all he said. This
is what Homer also intended when he said:

> Nireus who from Syme . . .
> Nireus, son of Aglaia . . .
> Nireus, of all the Greeks . . . .[2]

If you say much about a character it is necessary to mention
him often; hence if a name is often mentioned, we assume

1414 a

[2] This too became a favorite example of asyndeton in later critics. The
lines occur in the Catalogue of Ships, *Iliad* 2.671-4:

> Nireus from Syme brought three curved ships,
> Nireus, son of Aglaia and of Charopus,
> Nireus, most beautiful of all the Greeks
> Who came to Troy, saving Achilles only.

that much is said of him, so that in this case a character who is mentioned only once assumes greater importance by making use of this fallacy, and Homer makes us remember Nireus, though he is never mentioned again.

Three Kinds of Rhetoric

The style of deliberative or political oratory is in all respects like a sketched outline; the greater the crowd, the greater the distance from which the speech is judged, so that precision of detail is superfluous and indeed a bad thing, in the speech as in the sketch. Forensic style is more precise, especially before one judge, where there is least opportunity for rhetorical display; the judge grasps the nature of the whole case, the irrelevant and the contentious are out of place, and the decision is purely judicial. The same speakers do not achieve an equal reputation in all these different styles; there is least room for precision where delivery is of most importance, that is, where the voice has most scope, especially a loud voice.

The style of epideictic or display oratory is most like written prose, for its function is to be read. Next comes forensic oratory. It is superfluous to make further distinctions, into the pleasant style and the magnificent. Why should it have these qualities more than moderation or liberality or any other quality of character? The qualities we have already discussed will make the style pleasant, if indeed we have correctly defined the excellence of style. Why else should it be clear, not common but appropriate? Verbosity does not make for clarity, neither does brevity, but clearly the mean is right. So the qualities we have mentioned will, if they are well mixed, make the style pleasing: a mixture of current and unusual language, rhythm, and appropriateness will make it persuasive. So much for style, all kinds in general and every kind in particular, and we must now pass on to the arrangement of the speech.

Brief Summary of Chapters XIII-XIX

The rest of the book (chs. 13-19) deals with the third subject of study announced in the first chapter, namely, the arrangement of the different parts of a speech, and properly belongs to the history of rhetoric in the strict sense. Aristotle first establishes the essential parts of a speech. He himself would be satisfied with two parts: the statement of the thesis and the proof of it. He is willing, however, to allow four parts, namely, the pro-oemium or exordium, the prothesis or statement, the pistis or proof (which includes refutation), the epilogos or peroration, but no more. He ridicules the excessive subdivisions of contemporary rhetoricians and their fancy terminology, and then proceeds, in the following chapters, to analyze the purpose of each of his four sections, and the various means and devices by which this purpose can be attained in each of the three types of oratory, the forensic, the deliberative and the epideictic.

The exordium should make the purpose of the speaker clear; beyond that, however, it is used to get the audience into the right frame of mind, and digressions may be allowed. Though only the essential function of the exordium, i.e., to make one's purpose clear, is important to him, Aristotle goes on to list the various ways in which the audience may be influenced, and the commonplaces that may be used with this end in view (15). He then goes on to the statement or narrative (*diégésis*) and ridicules the popular notion that this should be brief: "As the customer said to the baker who asked him whether he wanted his bread hard or soft: 'Can't you bake it just right?'", and shows how the narrative should be dealt with in the different kinds of oratory. Chapter 17 deals with the different kinds of proofs and chapter 18 with rhetorical questions. The function of the peroration (19) is to dispose the hearer in one's favor once again, to amplify one's own position, to depreciate that of one's opponent, and to recapitulate the most important of one's arguments.

BIOGRAPHICAL INDEX

ACHILLES, Greek hero of the *Iliad* who retires in anger from the battle until, roused by the death of his friend Patroclus, he fights and kills Hector.

AEGEUS, legendary king of Athens. Aristotle condemns his sudden appearance in the *Medea* of Euripides as a coincidence neither probable nor inevitable (*Poet.* 25).

AEGISTHUS, in legend son of Thyestes and enemy of Agamemnon, was the paramour of Clytemnestra, ruled with her during the king's absence in Troy, and helped her murder her husband on his return. He was killed by Orestes.

AENEAS, son of Aphrodite and Peleus, was a Trojan hero in the *Iliad* and later the hero of Virgil's *Aeneid*.

AESCHYLUS (525-456 B.C.), the eldest of the three great tragedians. His plays raise deep religious and human problems. The tempo and language of his tragedies (seven remain) were already archaic by the late fifth century.

AESION (4th c. B.C.), Athenian orator and politician.

AGAMEMNON, king of Argos, commander in chief of the Greek forces before Troy in the *Iliad*. Having sacrificed his daughter Iphigenia to secure a favorable voyage for the fleet, he was, on his return from Troy, murdered by his wife Clytemnestra and her paramour Aegisthus.

AGATHON (*c.* 440-401 B.C.), Athenian writer of tragedies, younger contemporary of Euripides. He is satirized by Aristophanes as beautiful and effeminate. Agathon appears in Plato's *Symposium,* where his diction is beautiful but the content of his speech undistinguished. Aristotle says he introduced the drama of pure fiction (*Poet.* 9) and that he originated the choral interlude (*Poet.* 18), and criticizes him for "epic" plots.

AJAX, Greek hero in the *Iliad,* went mad and killed himself after the arms of the dead Achilles were awarded to Odysseus. This story is dramatized in Sophocles' *Ajax.*

ALCIBIADES (*c.* 450-404 B.C.), Athenian general, ambitious and unscrupulous, who betrayed his country to the Spartans. He was reinstated toward the end of the Peloponnesian war, but later had to take refuge with the Persians.

ALCIDAMAS (late 5th-early 4th c. B.C.), Sophist and rhetorician. A short treatise of his on the advisability of speaking impromptu is extant. He is criticized by Aristotle for "frigid" and excessive use of epithets (*Rh*. 3. 3).

ALCMAEON, in legend the son of Amphiaraus at whose command he killed his mother Eriphyle and was, like Orestes, pursued by the Furies.

ANAXANDRIDES (4th c. B.C.), writer of comedies in Athens.

ANDROTION (*c.* 416-346 B.C.), Athenian politician, pupil of Isocrates, wrote on the history of Athens.

ANTIGONE, daughter of Oedipus, who insists on giving her brother burial rites in spite of king Creon's edict that, as a traitor, he shall remain unburied (see Sophocles' *Antigone*).

ANTIMACHUS of Claros (mid-5th c. B.C.), epic poet and author of a *Thebaid*.

ANTINOUS, the legendary king of the Phaeacians in whose palace Odysseus tells the story of his wanderings.

ANTISTHENES (*c.* 455-360 B.C.), companion of Socrates and philosophic writer. He is often regarded as the founder of Cynic philosophy.

APHRODITE, the Greek goddess of sexual love, wife of Hephaestus, also mother of Eros.

APOLLO, god of light and of the sun, patron of music and the arts.

ARCHIDAMUS, mentioned in *Rhet*. 3. 4, is possibly the Spartan king of that name who reigned 360-338 B.C.

ARCHYTAS, of Tarentum (*fl.* early 4th c. B.C.), mathematician, engineer, and Pythagorean philosopher, is considered the founder of mechanics.

ARES, god of war.

ARIPHRADES, mentioned *(Poet.* 22) as ridiculing the precious language of poets. Little else is known about him.

ARISTOPHANES (*c.* 450-383 B.C.), Athenian writer of comedies of which eleven are extant, the only examples of Old Comedy we possess.

ASTYDAMAS, the name of both a father and son who wrote tragedies in Athens in the 4th century B.C. The reference in the *Poetics* (14) is probably to the son.

ATHENA, goddess of the arts and crafts, patron goddess of Athens.

BRYSON (4th c. B.C.), a Sophist and also a mathematician who attempted to square the circle.

CALLIPIDES (4th c. B.C.), Athenian actor.

CARCINUS (4th c. B.C.), Athenian writer of tragedies; he was notorious for his obscurity (*Poet.* 16, 17).

CEPHISODOTUS, referred to in *Rhet*. 3. 4, might possibly be the sculptor (early 4th c. B.C.), father of the more famous Athenian general and politician of the same name mentioned in *Rhet*. 3. 10.

CHABRIAS (d. 357 B.C.), a professional soldier often in the service of Athens.

CHAEREMON (4th c. B.C.), a writer of tragedies of whom Aristotle tells us that he mixed all meters and that his plays were more suitable for reading than acting (*Poet.* 1 and *Rhet.* 3. 12).

CHARES (mid-4th c. B.C.), Athenian general, military leader against Philip of Macedon.

CHIONIDES (5th c. B.C.), early writer of comedies in Athens (*Poet.* 3).

CHRYSES, father of Chryseis who comes to ransom his daughter from the Greeks at the beginning of the *Iliad*.

CICERO, MARCUS TULLIUS (106-43 B.C.), Roman statesman, philosopher, and orator, the champion of Roman humanism.

CLEON (d. 422 B.C.) succeeded Pericles as democratic and imperialist leader of the Athenian people. He is represented in Aristophanes and Thucydides as a tough and violent character.

CLEOPHON (4th c. B.C.), an Athenian writer of tragedies. Aristotle notes his realism (*Poet.* 2), the lack of dignity of his language (*Poet.* 22), and that he at times used dignified language inappropriately (*Rhet.* 3. 7).

CLYTEMNESTRA, wife of Agamemnon. Infuriated by the sacrifice of Iphigenia, she lived with Aegisthus while Agamemnon was at Troy, then killed him on his return. She was herself slain by her son Orestes.

CRATES (*fl.* 450 B.C.), Athenian writer of comedies. Aristotle says he was the first in Athens to write comedies with plots (*Poet.* 5).

CREON, brother of Iocasta, the mother and wife of Oedipus. He became king of Thebes after Oedipus' downfall.

CROESUS, last king (560-546 B.C.) of Lydia, was overthrown by the Persians. He was friendly to the Greeks and renowned for his wealth.

CYCLOPS, the man-eating, one-eyed giant blinded by Odysseus and his companions in the ninth book of the *Odyssey*.

DANAUS, in mythology, father of fifty daughters who were compelled to marry the fifty sons of Aegyptus. He advised them to kill their husbands, which all but one did. The Danaids were condemned in Hades to fill with water jars with holes in the bottom.

DEMETRIUS, the author of a treatise *On Style*, traditionally believed to be Demetrius of Phalerum who ruled Athens 317-307 B.C. and later went to Alexandria. This authorship is now rejected by most scholars and the treatise is usually dated in the 1st c. A.D.

DEMOCRATES (4th c. B.C.), Athenian orator.

DEMOCRITUS of Chios (5th c. B.C.), a Greek musician.

DEMOSTHENES (384-322 B.C.), the greatest orator of Athens and the passionate defender of Athens against Philip of Macedon.

DICAEOGENES (prob. late 5th c. B.C.), tragic poet. Nothing is known of him beyond what Aristotle tells us in *Poet.* 16.

DIOGENES of Sinope (4th c. B.C.), the great Cynic philosopher who lived in a tub. He preached a return to "natural" life.

DIONYSIUS (5th c. B.C. ?), Greek painter. Aristotle notes his realism (*Poet.* 2).

DIONYSIUS CHALCUS, "the Brazen" (5th c. B.C.), Athenian poet of whom little is known (*Rhet.* 3. 2).

DIONYSIUS of Halicarnassus (1st c. B.C.), Greek historian and man of letters; his critical works are extant, as well as about half his *Roman Antiquities.* He lived in Rome 30-8 B.C.

DIONYSUS, son of Zeus and Semele, god of wine and ecstasy, and patron of drama. Both comedies and tragedies were performed at festivals in his honor.

DOLON, Trojan warrior who comes to spy on the Greek camp at night and is killed by Odysseus and Diomede (*Iliad* 10).

ELECTRA, daughter of Agamemnon and Clytemnestra who helped Orestes kill their mother to avenge their father. We have an *Electra* by Sophocles and one by Euripides. The *Choephorae* of Aeschylus also deals with the same subject.

EMPEDOCLES of Acragas, in Sicily (c. 493-433 B.C.), biologist and philosopher, expounded his physical theories in hexameter verses of which considerable fragments remain. He originated the theory of the four roots or elements—fire, air, water, and earth—and two causes of motion—love and hate (i.e., attraction and repulsion). He was also the head of the Sicilian medical school and one of the first rhetoricians.

EPICHARMUS of Megara, in Sicily (early 5th c. B.C.), an early writer of comedies. He is mentioned (*Poet.* 5) as having been the first to write proper comic drama, i.e., with a plot.

ERIPHYLE, in legend the wife of Amphiaraus, killed by her son Alcmaeon because she was responsible for his father's death.

EUCLIDES, the Elder, unknown critic referred to in *Poet.* 22.

EUMAEUS, in the *Odyssey* loyal swineherd in whose cottage Odysseus takes refuge on his return to Ithaca.

EURIPIDES (c. 485-406 B.C.), the youngest of the three great tragedians, often called the philosopher of the stage. Aristotle calls him "the most tragic" of the poets (*Poet.* 13), though he is critical of him in other respects. We have eighteen of his plays.

EURYPYLUS, in legend son of Telephus.

EUXENUS, referred to in *Rhet.* 3. 4, is otherwise unknown.

GANYMEDE, in myth a Trojan youth. Zeus, attracted by his

beauty, snatched him up to Olympus to be cupbearer among the gods.

GLAUCON, the critic referred to in *Poet.* 25, might be the brother of Plato, or may be the Glaucon of Teos mentioned in *Rhet.* 3. 1 who wrote on delivery. Nothing is known of their works.

GORGIAS of Leontini (*c.* 483-376 B.C.), famous Sophist and teacher of rhetoric, only fragments of whose works remain. A pioneer, he was known for his exaggerated rhythms, antitheses, and farfetched metaphors, but he had very great influence.

HAEMON, son of Creon, king of Thebes, who threatens to kill his father when the latter insists on the punishment of Antigone in Sophocles' play.

HECTOR, son of Priam, king of Troy, and the main defender of his city. He is killed by Achilles.

HEGEMON of Thasos (prob. early 4th c. B.C.), a writer of comedies. When Aristotle calls him the originator of parodies (*Poet.* 2) he must mean that he first established parody as a separate genre.

HELLE, in myth, daughter of Athamas, threatened by her stepmother Ino, escaped on winged ram of the golden fleece, but fell into the sea thenceforth called the Hellespont.

HERACLES, son of Zeus and the mortal Alcmene. The legend of his twelve labors made him a symbol of suffering humanity.

HERACLITUS of Ephesus (*fl.* 500 B.C.), philosopher who stressed the flux of all the physical world, the chief though everchanging element being fire, and the only constant being the balance in change.

HERODOTUS (5th c. B.C.), the first great Greek historian. His history of the Greek struggle against Persia, in nine books, is extant.

HESIOD, a Boeotian poet of unknown date, but later than Homer. He wrote in hexameters: a didactic poem *Works and Days* (a farmer's calendar), and the *Theogony,* on the births and functions of the gods.

HIPPIAS of Thasos, another writer of whom we know no more than Aristotle tells us (*Poet.* 25).

HOMER, author of the two great epics of Greece, the *Iliad* and the *Odyssey,* and *the* poet for two thousand years. His date is uncertain, possibly 800 B.C.

ICARIUS, father of Penelope, wife of Odysseus.

IDRIEUS, Carian prince.

IPHICRATES (*c.* 415-353 B.C.), Athenian general who took part in most campaigns in the first half of the 4th c. B.C.

IPHIGENIA, in legend daughter of Agamemnon, who sacrificed her to Artemis to obtain a safe voyage to Troy (as in Euripides' *Iphigenia at Aulis*). Saved by the goddess, she becomes her priestess in distant Tauris where she must sacrifice all strangers. Her brother Orestes and his friend Pylades arrive and are captured. The story of their escape is told by Euripides in *Iphigenia in Tauris*.

ISOCRATES (436-388 B.C.), the most famous teacher of his day, taught rhetoric in his school in Athens for over fifty years.

IXION, in legend a Thessalian who tried to win the love of Hera and was, in the underworld, tied to an ever-revolving wheel.

LAIUS, king of Thebes, father of Oedipus.

LEPTINES (4th c. B.C.), Athenian, contemporary of Demosthenes.

LICYMNIUS (late 5th c. B.C.), a writer of dithyrambs who also wrote on the art of speech (*Rhet.* 3. 2); his work was apparently more suitable for reading than acting (*Rhet.* 3. 12) and he invented ridiculous subdivisions of a speech (*Rhet.* 3. 13).

LYCOPHRON. The reference in *Rhet.* 3. 3 is to a Sophist and writer of the 4th c. B.C., not to the better-known poet who was not born till later.

LYCOPHRON, mentioned in *Rhet.* 3. 9, with his brother Pitholaus murdered Alexander, tyrant of Pherae in 358 B.C.

LYNCEUS, in legend (a) one of the Argonauts who went to seek the Golden Fleece; (b) husband of Hypermnestra, the only one of the fifty daughters of Danaus who refused to murder her husband at the behest of their father.

MAGNES (early 5th c. B.C.), early writer of comedies in Athens, won the prize eleven times.

MEDEA, princess of Colchis who helped Jason to get the Golden Fleece and returned with him to Greece. Abandoned by him when he married the daughter of Creon, king of Corinth, she avenged herself on Jason by murdering her children by him (see the *Medea* of Euripides).

MELANIPPE, an Amazon queen of legend.

MELANIPPIDES of Melos (early 5th c. B.C.), writer of dithyrambs who gave up their strophic structure.

MELEAGER, a Calydonian hero who saved his lands from the Calydonian boar. His story is told in *Iliad* 9 to Achilles as an example of the futility of anger. He loved the virgin huntress Atalanta.

MENELAUS, king of Sparta, brother of Agamemnon, husband of Helen, and father of Hermione.

MEROPE, in legend, was compelled to marry Polyphontes, who had killed both her husband Cresphorites and two of her sons. The third son escaped and, returning secretly, managed to kill Polyphontes and recover the crown of Messene.

MNASITHEUS of Opuntium, singer of lyric poetry.

MOEROCLES (mid 4th c. B.C.), Athenian politician.

MYNNISCUS (4th c. B.C), Athenian actor.

NICERATUS, mentioned in *Rhet.* 3. 11, is unknown.

NICOCHARES (4th c. B.C.), Athenian writer of comedies, especially mythological burlesques.

NIOBE, in legend, mother of seven sons and seven daughters who boasted of her superior motherhood over Leto, mother of Apollo and Artemis. For this all her children were killed by them and she herself changed into a weeping column of stone.

NIREUS is mentioned only once in the *Iliad* as bringing a contingent of three ships from Syme.

ODYSSEUS, Greek hero before Troy in the *Iliad*. The *Odyssey* is the story of his adventures on his way back to Ithaca, his return being delayed by the anger of Poseidon.

OEDIPUS, son of Laius, king of Thebes, and of queen Iocasta. Ordered killed because of an oracle which foretold he would kill his father and marry his mother, he was exposed, then saved and brought up as their son by the king and queen of Corinth. In time, he unknowingly fulfills the oracle. His gradual discovery of the truth is the subject of Sophocles' famous tragedy.

ORESTES, in legend the son of Agamemnon and Clytemnestra. Leaving Argos after his mother's murder of Agamemnon, he returns to avenge his father and kills both his mother and her lover Aegisthus.

PALAMEDES, legendary Greek hero, of great astuteness and inventive skill, exposed Odysseus' feigned madness to avoid going to the Trojan war. Odysseus framed him on a charge of treachery and had him stoned to death.

PAUSON (5th c. B.C.?), a Greek painter of whom little is known. Aristotle suggests (*Poet.* 2) a hint of caricature in his works.

PEITHOLAUS (4th c. B.C.), Athenian orator and politician.

PELEUS, legendary king of Phthia, husband of the sea nymph Thetis and, by her, father of Achilles.

PENELOPE, wife of Odysseus who, though wooed by many suitors, loyally waits for Odysseus and is happily reunited with him in the end.

PERICLES (*c.* 500-429 B.C.), the leader of the Athenian democracy for the last thirty years of his life, re-elected strategos or general every year from 443 to 429.

PHILAMMON, mentioned in *Rhet.* 3. 11, is unknown, presumably a boxer.

PHILEMON, mentioned in *Rhet.* 3. 12, was a fourth-century actor.

PHILIP II (382-336 B.C.), king of Macedon from 359. He gradually brought the cities of Greece under his control and made possible the conquests of his son, Alexander the Great.

PHILOCTETES, Greek legendary hero, possessor of the bow of Heracles. He was abandoned in Lemnos by the Greeks on their way to Troy because of a disgusting wound. But because his bow was needed to take Troy, they had to seek him out many years later.

PHILOETIUS, shepherd of Odysseus to whom, together with Eumaeus, he makes himself known.

PHILOXENUS of Cythera (436-380 B.C.), writer of dithyrambs, lived in Syracuse.

PHINEUS, legendary king of Salmydessus on the Euxine, persuaded to blind his children by their stepmother.

PHORCYS, a Greek god of the sea, father of the Graiae, the Gorgons, and Scylla.

PHORMIS (early 5th c. B.C.), Sicilian writer of comedies, mostly on mythological subjects.

PINDARUS (4th c. B.C.), Athenian actor.

PITHOLAUS, with his brother Lycophron murdered Alexander of Pherae in 358 B.C.

PLATO (429-347 B.C.), disciple of Socrates and teacher of Aristotle, founded the Academy which had a continuous history till all pagan schools were closed in 529 A.D. His philosophical dialogues are extant. His own critical theories are found in the *Phaedrus,* the *Republic* (Books 3 and 10) and the second Book of the *Laws.*

POLYEUCTUS (mid 4th c. B.C.), Athenian politician and orator.

POLYGNOTUS (*fl.* 460 B.C.), a famous painter who lived in Athens. His pictures were of violent action and he was known for his success in rendering character in the human face (*Poet.* 6).

POLYIDUS, unknown beyond the references in *Poet.* 16 and 17.

POSEIDON, god of the sea, brother of Zeus. His anger delayed Odysseus' return home.

PRATYS, a rhapsode or reciter of epic poetry.

PROMETHEUS, the Titan who stole fire from Zeus to benefit mankind and was chained to a rock while an eagle daily devoured his liver. See Aeschylus' *Prometheus Bound.*

PROTAGORAS (*c.* 485-415 B.C.), most successful of all Sophists and teachers of rhetoric; his best-known sayings are that man is the measure of all things and that there are two sides to every question.

PYLADES, in legend the friend of Orestes who accompanied him on his wanderings.

RHADAMANTHUS, son of Zeus and Europa who acted as judge of the dead in the underworld.

SCYLLA, mythical daughter of Phorcys and Hecate, loved by Poseidon, turned by her rival Amphitrite into a sea monster which devoured those who sailed by (*Odyssey* 12).

SIMONIDES (556-468 B.C.), a famous writer of lyric and elegiac poetry, an older contemporary of Pindar.

SINON, left behind by the Greeks

at Troy to persuade the Trojans to take the wooden horse into the city.

SISYPHUS, mythical king of Corinth, was condemned in Hades to roll up a hill a large stone which always rolled down again just as it reached the top.

SOCRATES (469-399 B.C.), Athenian philosopher, insisted on the need to define one's terms, on self-knowledge, the identity of virtue with knowledge, and education by question and answer. He was executed for atheism and "corrupting the young." A whole Socratic literature arose after his death, conversations and dialogues by friends and disciples, notably Xenophon and Plato.

SOPHOCLES (c. 496-406 B.C.), the second and perhaps the most poetical of the three great Athenian writers of tragedy. Aristotle is especially appreciative of his *Oedipus King*. Seven of his plays are extant.

SOPHRON of Syracuse (c. 470-400 B.C.), a writer of mimes, i.e., short sketches from daily life in rhythmical prose. Only very brief fragments remain.

SOSISTRATUS, well-known rhapsode or reciter of epic poems.

STESICHORUS of Himera in Sicily (c. 632-556 B.C.), a famous writer of lyric poetry with a strong narrative element.

STHENELUS (5th c. B.C.), writer of tragedies, is criticized by Aristotle (*Poet.* 22) for his commonplace language. He is also ridiculed by the comic poets.

TELEGONUS, in post-Homeric legend the son of Odysseus by Circe. He unwittingly kills his father.

TELEMACHUS, the son of Odysseus and Penelope. At the beginning of the *Odyssey* he sets out to find news of his father, and then helps him on his return to take vengeance on the suitors.

TELEPHUS, mythological king of the Mysians and son of Heracles. Wounded by Achilles, he is told by an oracle that only Achilles can cure him. His visit to the Greek camp disguised as a beggar was the subject of a lost play of Euripides much ridiculed by comic poets.

TERPANDER of Lesbos (early 7th c. B.C.), musician and poet, wrote nomes which were a type of hymn accompanied by music on the lyre.

THEODAMAS, referred to in *Rhet.* 3. 4, is otherwise unknown.

THEODECTES (c. 375-334 B.C.), orator and writer of tragedies in Athens. Only fragments of his work remain.

THEODORUS of Byzantium, a writer on rhetoric and teacher in the late 5th and early 4th centuries.

THESEUS, legendary king of Athens and friend of Heracles.

THRASYMACHUS of Chalcedon (*fl.* 430-400 B.C.), Sophist and teacher of rhetoric, known for his ability to rouse the emotions of his audience and for developing a prose as against a poetic diction.

THYESTES, in legend the son of

Pelops and brother of Atreus. The rivalry between the brothers is illustrated by many stories, including that in which Atreus serves Thyestes his own children's flesh at a banquet. Atreus is the father of Agamemnon and Thyestes the father of Aegisthus.

TIMOTHEUS of Miletus (c. 450-360 B.C.), a writer of dithyrambs. Some considerable fragments remain.

TYDEUS, in legend the son of Oeneus, king of Calydon, and father of Diomede who is a Greek hero in the *Iliad*.

XENARCHUS, son of Sophron, apparently wrote mimes, like his father, but very little is known about him.

XENOPHANES of Colophon (c. 570-460 B.C.), poet and philosopher, author of satires and elegiac poems of which only fragments remain.

XENOPHON (c. 430-354 B.C.), friend of Socrates, soldier, country gentleman, writer of historical, Socratic, and moral works, many of which are extant.

XERXES, king of Persia 485-465 B.C., who invaded Greece. On his way he bridged the Hellespont and dug a canal through the peninsula of Mount Athos.

ZEUS, the greatest of the gods, brother of Hera, Hades, and Poseidon, and father of the other gods.

ZEUXIS (late 5th c. B.C.), a famous Greek painter of Italian birth; did not try to represent character (*Poet.* 6) but idealized his models (*Poet.* 25).